29.00

ASHE Higher Education Report: Volume 34, Number 6
Kelly Ward, Lisa E. Wolf-Wendel, Series Editors

D1104352

The Development of Doctoral Students: Phases of Challenge and Support

Susan K. Gardner

The Development of Doctoral Students: Phases of Challenge and Support
Susan K. Gardner
ASHE Higher Education Report: Volume 34, Number 6
Kelly Ward, Lisa E. Wolf-Wendel, Series Editors

ISSN 1551-6970   electronic ISSN 1554-6306   ISBN 978-0-4705-0904-3

The ASHE Higher Education Report is part of the Jossey-Bass Higher and Adult Education Series and is published six times a year by Wiley Subscription Services, Inc., A Wiley Company, at Jossey-Bass, 989 Market Street, San Francisco, California 94103-1741.

For subscription information, see the Back Issue/Subscription Order Form in the back of this volume.

CALL FOR PROPOSALS: Prospective authors are strongly encouraged to contact Kelly Ward (kaward@wsu.edu) or Lisa Wolf-Wendel (lwolf@ku.edu). See "About the ASHE Higher Education Report Series" in the back of this volume.

Visit the Jossey-Bass Web site at **www.josseybass.com.**

Printed in the United States of America on acid-free recycled paper.

The ASHE Higher Education Report is indexed in CIJE: Current Index to Journals in Education (ERIC), Current Abstracts (EBSCO), Education Index/Abstracts (H.W. Wilson), ERIC Database (Education Resources Information Center), Higher Education Abstracts (Claremont Graduate University), IBR & IBZ: International Bibliographies of Periodical Literature (K.G. Saur), and Resources in Education (ERIC).

Advisory Board

Contents

Executive Summary

Student development theory has become a central tenet of the work of student affairs administrators, the main foundation for many graduate programs in higher education, and a driving force behind many contemporary efforts and movements in higher education today. Student development theory, however, has primarily been concerned with undergraduate college students. Conspicuously missing from the literature on student development theory is development of graduate students. Graduate students make up a large part of the higher education student population, totaling more than 2.1 million students in 2004, with the doctoral student population estimated at nearly 400,000. Doctoral students are educated at U.S. institutions of higher education to become tomorrow's scholars, researchers, leaders, and educators. Taken together, a better understanding of the developmental needs, challenges, and issues facing doctoral students is certainly warranted.

The existing literature about the doctoral student experience focuses mainly on the academic and professional aspects of the experience and rarely, if ever, addresses any of the personal development evidenced in the student throughout the degree program. Second, the existing literature generally treats doctoral students as only those who matriculate full time through their programs directly after their undergraduate experience and tends not to focus on part-time or professional doctoral students, a growing population in U.S. graduate education. Although these populations are faced with distinct programmatic and academic experiences in their disciplinary programs, this monograph focuses on the larger issues of development that occur during the doctoral experience. Accordingly, the theory discussed in this monograph applies to adult development, psychology, sociology, and education to synthesize the existing literature on student and adult development and to suggest areas for future research and theory.

Why Is the Suggested Topic Important to Higher Education?

The focus on graduate education and the doctoral student experience in higher education has increased in the past several years. In particular, many have decried the high rates of attrition among doctoral programs in the United States, as only a little more than 50 percent of all doctoral students entering their programs complete the degree. To address the issue of attrition in doctoral education, many studies and initiatives have been developed to better understand the causes and consequences of doctoral student attrition.

Although the study of undergraduate student development has become a major part of understanding attrition, retention, and student satisfaction, this same understanding has not yet been extended to the doctoral student population in higher education. Development, of course, does not cease at graduation from college but extends throughout one's life. By understanding how the graduate experience influences doctoral students' development, higher education constituencies may also understand how to best assist students through developmentally challenging periods of their educational experience. This understanding may subsequently play a role in stemming the attrition of doctoral students.

In addition, much like the research on college student development assists practitioners and scholars in better understanding the populations with which they work, a better understanding of the development of the doctoral student population will assist higher education professionals in best serving the needs of this constantly growing and changing demographic in colleges and universities.

This monograph seeks to fill the existing gap in the literature by examining the extant literature regarding doctoral students, student development, adult development and learning, and the overall doctoral experience. This literature is presented in a three-phase framework of graduate education, itself assisting in understanding the developmental nature of the graduate student experience in the United States.

The Three Phases of Doctoral Education

Using Sanford's (1966) concept of challenge and support, the monograph presents a three-phase model of development at the doctoral level. The first phase consists of the time of admission to the program through the beginning year of coursework. It is marked by a transition from the undergraduate experience to the more advanced expectations of graduate work and the formation of relationships with peers and faculty in the program. The second phase of the graduate program includes the time spent mainly in coursework until the examination period; it is also characterized by deepening relationships with peers and faculty and the formation of a more professional relationship with the faculty advisor. The third phase marks the culmination of coursework through the dissertation research, that is, the period generally referred to as "candidacy." In this phase, students begin to transition away from their student role to a more professional role, particularly in their professional endeavors. The model is therefore based on developmental and interpersonal experiences rather than only chronology, again accounting for differences between full-time and part-time status. The chapters addressing these phases incorporate qualitative data from the research conducted with nearly 200 doctoral students at multiple institutions to illustrate these phases and the dynamics at play in them.

Foreword

How college students grow and change is a topic of great interest to researchers and practitioners in higher education. Facilitating the positive, holistic growth of students is, in fact, an explicit goal of many who work in higher education. Yet in the writings about college student development, we seem to have left out an exploration of the process by which some of our students develop. Indeed, when reading the college student development literature, it is clear that the focus remains on traditional-aged, full-time college students. We have diversified the samples of many studies to represent the diversity of students on our campuses, but as a field we have really not grappled substantially with the needs of "other" students who do not fit the mold of what we consider "typical." Graduate students are one of those groups about whom we know little, especially with regard to their personal and professional development.

Researchers and practitioners have not yet thoroughly examined the developmental needs of graduate students for many reasons. Unlike undergraduates, who have student affairs professions to champion their cause, typically no such institutionwide champions exist for graduate education. It might also be that we think of graduate students as fully developed or that we assume their development is beyond our capacity to facilitate. Perhaps they have not been studied from a developmental perspective because they do not fit as easily into a single mold of experience as do traditional-aged students. Although these concerns may be real, the present monograph presents a convincing argument that it is time for those of us who work in higher education to more explicitly consider the educational and developmental needs of our graduate students. This monograph takes an important first step in this direction by examining the development of doctoral students.

Susan Gardner uses this monograph to make a strong case that we should care about the development of graduate students in general and doctoral students in particular. She explains that their success or failure is strongly connected to the future of higher education and that financial implications for students, institutions, and society exist if we fail to consider the holistic needs of graduate students. She also makes the case that for moral and ethical reasons we should care about the success and development of doctoral students. It is true that doctoral experiences vary greatly by academic discipline, by institution, by students' circumstances, and by their career aspirations. These important distinctions are noted and explained carefully in the monograph. At the same time, this monograph finds important commonalities in the doctoral student experience and provides helpful information to institutions, schools, departments, and faculty on how best to facilitate the success of their doctoral students and pay heed to their developmental needs.

One of the most helpful pieces of this monograph is its "primer" on student development theory. For those who are not yet familiar with these theories or who are seeking a refresher, this review is exceedingly helpful. The review of student development theories also offers a strong conceptual framework for the material presented in the monograph. This monograph is also helpful because it breaks down the doctoral experience into several phases, providing a strong and clear understanding of what developmental needs and milestones might be most salient at key points of the doctoral student experience. The use of interviews to augment the existing literature brings life to the monograph and makes it readable, while also making the arguments in the monograph more compelling and personal.

This monograph is useful for a number of audiences. Doctoral students who read this monograph are likely to benefit from seeing that their concerns are "normal" and survivable. Faculty advisors who seek the means and resources to more effectively help their students reach their goals will also find this monograph useful. Further, the monograph is helpful to student affairs and graduate-level administrators who might oversee programs or policies for graduate students. Understanding the developmental needs of doctoral students may improve such programs and yield positive results for all involved. Last, this monograph might be useful to higher education scholars as they seek to expand the theories and research on student development.

This monograph offers an accessible, thoughtful analysis of an important topic. It helps us to better understand the needs and experiences of doctoral students and reminds us that this group of students needs our attention and understanding.

Kelly Ward
Series Editor

Acknowledgments

The writing process for this monograph has been one of challenge and support. I appreciate those friends and colleagues who provided helpful feedback in the first iterations of the project, including Pilar Mendoza, Karri Holley, and Tricia Bertram Gallant. I also thank colleagues and graduate students who have assisted in data collection over the years and have assisted me in publishing and presenting these studies: Michael Hayes, Cheryl Frugé, Xyanthe Neider, G. Todd Vanek, Benita Barnes, Dorian McCoy, and Tam Le. Ted Greenwood at the Sloan Foundation was one of the first to believe in me, and I appreciate the funding assistance provided by Sloan that began this journey. Tremendous thanks are due to Lisa Wolf-Wendel, who has been a supportive editor throughout my many iterations of this process. My unending love and gratitude go to my supportive partner and best friend, Thom Cosgrove, who not only gave me early comments but also provided the support I needed throughout the process. And my mother, Patricia Gardner, has always been my biggest fan and supporter. Finally, I wish to extend my deepest appreciation and admiration to the doctoral students I have interviewed, instructed, advised, and met over the years. Each of you is a tremendous inspiration to what I do each day.

Published online in Wiley InterScience
(www.interscience.wiley.com) • DOI: 10.1002/aehe.3406

The Development of Doctoral Students: Phases of Challenge and Support

IN 1905, THE PRESIDENT OF THE UNIVERSITY OF CHICAGO, William Harper, predicted the evolution of student development: "In order that the student may receive the assistance so essential to his highest success, another step in the onward evolution will take place. This step will be *the scientific study of the student himself.* In the time that is coming provision must be made, either by the regular instructors or by those appointed especially for the purpose, to study in detail the man or woman to whom instruction is offered" (p. 321).

Specifically, Harper called for an examination of the college student's character, intellectual capacity and characteristics, and social nature, specifically with the aim to assist the student in a selection of studies, career path, and the formation of character. He foretold, "This feature of twentieth-century college education will come to be regarded as of greatest importance, and fifty years hence will prevail as widely as it is now lacking" (p. 325).

More than a century later, the higher education community finds itself immersed in a multitude of theories and research that assist us in explaining, interpreting, understanding, and even predicting college students' behavior, cognition, aspirations, and attitudes, rightly affirming Harper's prediction (1905). Defined as "the ways that a student grows, progresses, or increases his or her developmental capabilities as a result of enrollment in an institution of higher education" (Rodgers, 1990, p. 27), student development has become the central tenet of the work of student affairs administrators (American Council on Education, 1949), the main foundation for many graduate programs in higher education (Komives and Taub, 2000), and a driving force behind many contemporary efforts and movements in higher education (Evans, Forney, and Guido-DiBrito, 1998).

Student development theory, however, has primarily been concerned with the undergraduate college student experience (McEwen, 2003). Conspicuously missing from the literature base on student development theory is the development pertaining to graduate students. Graduate students make up a large part of the higher education student population, totaling more than 2.2 million students in 2006 with a predicted enrollment of 2.6 million by 2017 (Planty and others, 2008). Doctoral students, in particular, represent approximately 18 percent of the total graduate student population (Walker and others, 2008) and are educated at institutions of higher education to become tomorrow's scholars, researchers, leaders, and educators in social, governmental, educational, biomedical, business, and industrial organizations (Council of Graduate Schools, 2005). Despite this importance, doctoral students' development is rarely, if ever, addressed in the literature.

Why Do We Need to Understand Doctoral Students' Development?

In the past decade, focus has increased on graduate education and the doctoral student experience in higher education. In particular, many have decried the high rates of attrition among doctoral programs in the United States, as only a little more than 50 percent of all doctoral students entering their programs will complete the degree (Council of Graduate Schools, 2008). This rate is disconcerting when one considers the economic, social, and personal consequences of doctoral student attrition (Bowen and Rudenstine, 1992; Lovitts, 2001). In particular, the higher education community should be concerned about doctoral student attrition for four main reasons.

First, doctoral student attrition is extremely expensive for institutions; these expenses begin to accrue even before students begin their program. For example, recruiting new students is much more costly than retaining students (Lau, 2003), especially when one considers the amount of time expended by individual faculty members contacting and making connections with prospective students, the materials and resources that are purchased and distributed to recruit students, and the amount of money needed for events such as campus visits and recruiting days. Once admitted, full-time students are often granted assistantships that pay the students' tuition and provide a stipend. For students who leave before completing the degree program, this money is, for all intents and purposes, lost. In its study of doctoral student attrition, the University of Notre Dame found that it would save one million dollars a year in stipends alone if attrition went down by 10 percent (Smallwood, 2004). Moreover, as Nettles and Millett (2006) point out, "Doctoral programs may be the most loosely structured and individually tailored of all higher education degrees" (p. 225), and this individual tailoring is indeed expensive.

Second, doctoral student attrition has social consequences. Those who receive doctorates may go on to become talented leaders, innovative researchers, prolific scholars, and influential educators in both the United States and abroad. A large percentage of the doctorates produced in the United States each year are conferred to those from other countries (Hoffer and others, 2006). With this scope of influence, understanding the students' experiences and structuring these experiences for success are vital to doctoral education's livelihood in this country. In the same vein, the lack of underrepresented populations in many fields, including those in the sciences, engineering, and mathematics, has become a matter of national concern (National Science Board, 2008). U.S. society and the larger world require innovative thinking in research fields to remain competitive (Council on Postsecondary Education, 2007), and colleges and universities require representative populations to educate students' everchanging demographics (Cross, 1996; Knowles and Harleston, 1997; National Science Foundation, 2004a).

Third, we should be concerned for personal reasons. Lovitts (2001) asserts, "The most important reason to be concerned about graduate student attrition is that it can ruin individuals' lives" (p. 6). Those students who seek to obtain a doctoral degree are certainly intelligent, capable individuals. "They are people who have been successful their entire lives and view themselves as superior students, as people who can surmount any academic obstacle, and as people who finish things they start" (p. 6). Many of those who leave doctoral programs do not do so positively. Often, they may leave and feel like "failures," perhaps influencing their future success in the job market or in their personal lives (Lovitts, 2001).

Therefore, although the study of student development has become a major part of understanding attrition, retention, and student satisfaction at the undergraduate level (Pascarella and Terenzini, 2005), this same application has not yet been extended to the doctoral student population in higher education. Through understanding how the graduate experience influences doctoral student development, the higher education community may also understand how to best assist students through developmentally challenging periods of their educational experience. Subsequently, this understanding may ultimately play a role in stemming doctoral student attrition overall.

Why Have Doctoral Students Been Forgotten?

Considering their importance and the need to understand them, why have doctoral students been absent in discussions of student development? Perhaps for several reasons: First are classic assumptions made about the doctoral student population. For example, although Harper (1905) was fervent in his call for more research on the college student more than a century ago, he compared the needs of the college student to the graduate or "university" student: "Here, in some degree, is the difference between college and university. The college is the place for the student to study and test himself . . . for the instructor to study each student, and to point out his weak and his strong points, that the former may be corrected and the latter still more greatly strengthened. The university is the place for men who have come to know themselves, and now have learned what they can do and what they cannot do, to study in the line of their chosen calling" (pp. 324–325).

Implicit in this quote is the assumption that the graduate student is completely self-aware and entirely developed upon entering graduate school, almost as if the development of the student ceases upon graduation from an undergraduate institution. Although this quote represents prevailing thought of more than one hundred years ago, one need only consider the most popular text used in student development theory courses today (Evans, Forney, and Guido-DiBrito, 1998) to see that not much has changed. Graduate students and their specific developmental issues and needs are noticeably absent in contemporary discussions of student development in higher education today.

Second, one might attribute the dearth of literature related to doctoral student development as owing to the assumption that the doctoral student is not merely a student, but rather a colleague, a professional, or even an equal to that of the faculty and administrators at the higher education institution (Katz and Hartnett, 1976), thereby dismissing the student's needs as a developing and growing individual. Often placed in professional positions such as graduate teaching and research assistants or serving full-time in professional roles outside graduate school, graduate students are perhaps, not surprisingly, no longer viewed in a student-like role.

Third, the focus of student development theory has predominately been the undergraduate student. Although we know that demographics of the "typical" college student are changing, most undergraduates can nevertheless be considered in the traditional framework: eighteen to twenty-two years old, residential, single, and full time. Doctoral students, however, do not fall into the traditional framework. Doctoral students may come directly from a bachelor's degree program or may begin their program midway through a professional career, they may be twenty-two or sixty-two (or any age in between), and they may have children or may even care for elderly parents. In other words, the absence of doctoral students in the developmental literature may owe greatly to the fact that doctoral students are anything but a homogeneous group. This lack of homogeneity can pose difficulties for theories that try to generalize to a larger population.

Fourth, the absence of literature relating to doctoral students and their development may reflect the dearth of literature about doctoral education in general. Until the past two decades, relatively little research was conducted on doctoral education despite the fact that the first doctorate was awarded in the United States in 1861 (Noble, 1994). In other words, although countless studies exist about undergraduate education and its student population, we still know relatively little about doctoral education in the United States. What we do know is generally more programmatic or structural in nature rather than the effects of doctoral education on students. As shown in Exhibit 1, much of the existing literature about doctoral education can be conceptualized in several broad categories.

Finally, we might attribute the lack of literature about doctoral student development to the evolution of the study of student development itself. In 1978, Knefelkamp, Widick, and Parker edited one of the first volumes on

EXHIBIT 1
Major Areas of Scholarship in Doctoral Education

Area of Scholarship	Major Authors
Doctoral student completion and attrition	Bowen and Rudenstine, 1992; Council of Graduate Schools, 2008; Golde, 2005; Lovitts, 2001; Nerad and Miller, 1996; Tinto, 1993
Time to degree	Abedi and Benkin, 1987; Baird, 1993; Ferrer de Valero, 2001
Socialization process	Antony, 2002; Austin, 2002; Baird, 1972; Ellis, 2001; Gonzalez, 2006; Margolis and Romero, 1998; Mendoza, 2007; Rosen and Bates,1967; Weidman, Twale, and Stein, 2001
Dissertation	Baird, 1997; Boote and Beile, 2005; Goodchild, Green, Katz, and Kluever, 1997; Isaac, Quinlan, and Walker, 1992
Advising roles and relationships	Aguinis and others, 1996; Baird, 1995; Bargar and Mayo-Chamberlain, 1983; Clark and Corcoran, 1986; Schroeder and Mynatt, 1993
Gender and race in the above categories	Cao, 2001; Ellis, 2001; Gonzalez and Marin, 2002; Green and Scott, 2003; Heinrich, 1995; Herzig, 2004a; Maher, Ford, and Thompson, 2004; National Research Council, 2001; Soto Antony and Taylor, 2004; Turner and Thompson, 1993
Disciplinary differences in the above categories	Crosby, 1996; Elkana, 2006; Gardner, 2007; Golde, 2005; Golde and Walker, 2006; Lott and Gardner, forthcoming; Walker and others, 2008

college student development. They discussed the evolution of student development theory as a body of literature that was relatively nonexistent in the early 1970s to one that was virtually exploding later in that same decade. Since then, we have seen countless theories, studies, and explorations of student development at the college level, and the existing body of literature continues to multiply each day. This is to say, if student development as a field of study did not emerge strongly until the late 1970s—or 340 years after the establishment of the first institution of higher education in the United States—perhaps it is not surprising that we have not begun a serious discussion of doctoral student development in the same right.

How Do Doctoral Students Develop?

Despite the lack of literature attesting to it, doctoral students do, of course, develop. Development, as we know, does not cease at graduation from college but extends throughout the lifespan (Erikson, 1959; Kuh and Thomas, 1983; Levinson, 1990; Merriam, 1984; Merriam and Clark, 2006). Moreover, doctoral students, although certainly capable and talented adults, are nevertheless still students. They seek the knowledge, skills, and habits of mind particular to their specific field of study through obtaining the doctoral degree (Walker and others, 2008). In the pursuit of this degree, doctoral students therefore develop as a result of and in relation to their educational goals.

More specifically, the doctoral education experience is one that the recent Carnegie Initiative on the Doctorate referred to as "a complex process of *formation*," a process that entails "not only the development of intellectual expertise but [also] the growth of the personality, character, habits of heart and mind, and the role that the given discipline is capable of and meant to play in academe and society at large" (Walker and others, 2008, p. 8). Given this explanation, the process of transformation that occurs in doctoral education influences much more than one's professional preparation; it also entails the development of the whole self.

Development at any level occurs as a result of two conditions: challenge and support (Sanford, 1966). According to Sanford, when individuals are presented with a challenging situation or experience that has not previously been encountered, a new response emerges, thereby resulting in development. If too many new situations emerge without the appropriate support to mitigate these challenges, however, the individual may actually digress in his or her development. Therefore, it is the optimum balance of challenge and support that underlies development.

At the doctoral level, sources of challenge abound. Students who enter a doctoral program for the first time face the new challenges of meeting their peers, proving their abilities to faculty, and becoming competent in their subject matter. As students progress, the challenges change, be it mastering coursework, passing a comprehensive examination, or completing a dissertation. Indeed, without the support of others, these challenges can become overwhelming. It is this conceptualization of challenge and support that guides the framework for this monograph, leading to a better understanding of doctoral student development.

A Model of Doctoral Student Development

Figure 1 illustrates the guiding model for this monograph. Created through multiple qualitative studies with 177 doctoral students from across the United States (see the appendix), the model presents the development of doctoral

Figure 1
Conceptual Framework

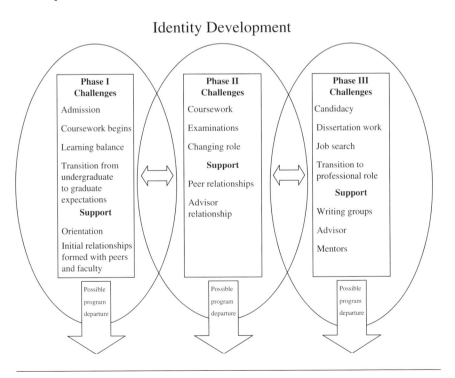

students as a series of three phases of challenge and support. This three-phase model is different from other scholars' explanations of the doctoral experience, as it is conceptualized in phases rather than stages. Stage models, according to King (1994), often assume a sequence of "lock-step fashion, one stage at a time, with no overlap between stages" (p. 417). This model of doctoral student development is not static. In other words, it is not suggested that events or interactions occur only during one phase but rather are fluid in nature, allowing for students to visit and revisit issues and opportunities throughout their programs.

Furthermore, the three-phase conceptualization is an addition to the current body of knowledge, as it addresses the doctoral experience from both the programmatic and developmental perspectives, which is to say that the model encompasses an understanding wherein the student not only changes professionally but also personally and interpersonally. This new conceptualization of the doctoral experience therefore focuses clearly on the developmental experiences of students rather than solely on programmatic turning points or stages of socialization.

The Phases of Doctoral Student Development

The three phases of the model, as shown in Figure 1, incorporate Phase I (Entry), Phase II (Integration), and Phase III (Candidacy), with overarching identity development or possible program departure occurring throughout these phases. Detailed explanations of the development that occurs in each phase are provided in subsequent chapters and outlined briefly below.

Phase I. Phase I is described as the time leading up to admission into the doctoral program until the period when coursework begins. This phase generally lasts only a few months but according to many students (Gardner, 2007, 2008a, 2008c) greatly affects the rest of their program, solidifies their decision to attend one institution over another, and even influences their decision to persist in doctoral education altogether. Phase I presents multiple challenges to the new student, including applying to prospective programs and institutions; submitting requisite materials to programs; visiting campuses; meeting and talking with faculty members, staff, and graduate students in those prospective programs; making a final decision about the program of choice;

moving to the new location; beginning their coursework; learning to balance the demands of life and graduate school; and understanding the changing expectations of their graduate student role. To mitigate these challenges, however, new doctoral students have several sources of support, including the fellow students they will meet during orientation, the faculty with whom they will connect and have in their initial courses, and the staff who provide support and direction through the beginning months.

Phase II. Phase II generally encompasses time in coursework but also represents much of the social and academic integration that students will experience as they progress toward candidacy. The challenges facing students in Phase II include demonstrating competency and skills first in their coursework and then through the examination process while also making the transition from being a knowledge consumer to a knowledge producer through research. Students are also challenged by the need to form deeper relationships with both peers and faculty. Supportive relationships with these individuals are therefore imperative to students' success and development in this phase.

Phase III. After moving through the challenges of Phase II, students move into the final phase of their doctoral experience. Phase III marks the period after which students have passed their examinations, or candidacy status. At this phase, students are faced with the daunting challenge of completing independent research for the dissertation and may also begin seeking professional positions. The support students have had in the past, whether through close peer relationships in coursework or daily interaction with faculty, may disappear, intensifying these challenges.

Identity Development

As students progress through the three phases, they also experience personal identity development in relation to the challenges and support that await them. As seen in Figure 1, the identity development that occurs is as fluid as the phases: the student may confront developmental challenges or issues that are directly related to the experiences in the three phases or may simply experience overarching development that occurs external to the doctoral student experience. Regardless, however, identity development continues throughout adulthood (Merriam and Clark, 2006).

The remaining chapters of the monograph make note of identity development that may occur as a result of the particular phase being discussed. For example, cognitive development that occurs as a result of coursework and the research experience, psychosocial development as the student becomes more competent in his or her subject matter, and identity development as the student confronts particular challenges that arise in his or her experiences. It is important to note, however, that not all development that occurs will be solely the result of the challenges and support that the three phases of the doctoral student experience offers but may transpire as a result of influences external to the program as well.

Student Departure

Not all students progress through all three phases of their doctoral experience. Doctoral student completion in the United States averages only around 50 percent (Council of Graduate Schools, 2008), and, depending on the discipline, completion rates may be even lower. For example, after seven years, only 24.7 percent of doctoral students in history will have graduated, whereas 69 percent of doctoral students in civil engineering will have completed their program in the same period of time (Council of Graduate Schools, 2008).

An exhaustive discussion of doctoral student attrition is not provided here (for a comprehensive treatment of doctoral student attrition, see Baird, 1993; Bowen and Rudenstine, 1992; Cook and Swanson, 1978; Council of Graduate Schools, 2008; Girves and Wemmerus, 1988; Golde, 2005; Golde and Dore, 2001; Lovitts, 2001; Nerad and Miller, 1996; Nettles and Millett, 2006). Instead, what follows in the remaining chapters is a discussion of the frequency and the effects attrition may have on the individual who departs the degree program. Specifically, the discussion addresses student departure as a result of overwhelming challenges or a paucity of support in each of the three phases.

Differences That Make a Difference

It is important to consider the diversity of the doctoral student population when one discusses the doctoral student experience. For example, the fact that years are not ascribed to the three-phase model was quite intentional, as not all students are enrolled full time and not all students uniformly complete requirements in the same time period. Moreover, owing to disciplinary differences, the amount of coursework required to complete a doctoral degree in one field and requirements for entrance into candidacy or for the dissertation may be substantially less than in another.

We also know that individual differences among students such as age and background greatly affect the scope and experience of students' development as well (Strange, 2005). Students' experiences prior to entering graduate school also affect their development, much as the experiences they have while in graduate school. We can surmise that many of the students entering a doctoral program may have dealt with significant developmental challenges before arriving but that the new environment of graduate school may require that students revisit these same developmental issues. It is important to keep in mind, however, that students are as diverse as their experiences and that these individual differences must be accounted for in any consideration of their overall development or change during graduate school.

Understanding the role the environment plays is an additional part of student development (Rodgers, 1990; Strange, 2005). In this way, the departmental and institutional contexts in which students are educated will also factor greatly into the scope of their development. Much like undergraduate education in this vein, a supportive departmental environment, as evidenced through supportive relationships among faculty, staff, and students, will play a much different role in students' development than an environment that is unaware of its students and that plays a passive role in the students' education (Gardner, 2008a).

Similarly, as the purpose and scope of doctoral degrees in particular disciplines vary widely, so may the scope of the development experienced by the student. Using again the example of social identity, students may continue to experience identity development regarding race, gender, sexual orientation, or their spirituality as a result of their doctoral experiences, perhaps through discussions or situations in coursework or in their research that challenge their development. Correspondingly, relationships with peers and with faculty members may result in psychosocial development such as interpersonal maturity.

In the context of each of the three phases, examples are provided to allow the reader to understand the differences in development that may occur as a result of these disciplinary differences as well as other differences that affect an individual student's development over time.

Organization of the Monograph

This monograph seeks to inform faculty, staff, administrators, and students about the nature of and structure in doctoral programs that lead to doctoral student development. It is accomplished through the remaining chapters, focusing first on an overview of existing student development theory and then on the structure of doctoral education and its role in the three phases of development. In other words, the remaining chapters provide an understanding of the *who* in doctoral education in the United States, followed by an understanding of the *what, why,* and *how* of students' development.

For those unfamiliar with the subject, the next chapter offers a brief primer on the topic of student development, including an overview of predominant theories in the field and how they pertain to doctoral student education in general.

"Understanding Doctoral Education" provides an explanation of doctoral education, its structure, and its constituencies. This chapter aims to offer readers a basic understanding of the history of doctoral education in the United States, the primary types of doctoral degrees, and an overview of the institutions that offer the doctorate as well as the students, faculty members, and administrators involved in the development of the student on a daily basis.

The subsequent three chapters detail the three phases of doctoral student development. Each of these chapters includes information about the specific challenges and support characteristic of the phase as well as quotes from qualitative interviews to demonstrate the development that occurs. "Phase I: Entry" encompasses the conceptualization of Phase I, including the time of admission and the first experiences in the graduate program. "Phase II: Integration" speaks to the second phase of the doctoral student experience. During this phase, students are in the midst of completing coursework and preparing for examinations, developing relationships with peers and faculty, and beginning to understand the professional role that they seek to obtain. "Phase III: Candidacy" addresses the last phase, including the time students spend in candidacy at the doctoral level or the culmination of their doctoral program. The final chapter culminates with an overview and summary of the framework and its implications for policy, practice, and further research.

Student Development Theory: A Primer

THE PURPOSE OF THIS CHAPTER is to provide an overview of existing theories of student development for those who may be unfamiliar with the area. Beginning with a definition of student development, the chapter then focuses on three areas of theory: psychosocial development, including professional and adult development; social identity development; and cognitive development. The chapter connects a discussion of these theories with the concept of doctoral student development.

Defining Student Development

Student development has been described as "the ways that a student grows, progresses, or increases his or her developmental capabilities as a result of enrollment in an institution of higher education" (Rodgers, 1990, p. 27). In general, development is about becoming a more complex individual (McEwen, 2005). The accompanying theory used to explain and understand student development allows educators to "proactively identify and address student needs, design programs, develop policies, and create healthy . . . environments that encourage positive growth in students" (Evans, Forney, and Guido-DiBrito, 1998, p. 5).

As previously mentioned, development occurs as a result of corresponding challenge and support. Sanford (1966) postulated that when students are faced with new challenges in their lives, a response or way to cope with the situation must emerge. If the challenge is positively resolved, this new response, view of life, or coping mechanism adds to the development of the student's identity. If negatively resolved, however, stress, anxiety, or dysfunctional behavior may result, which in effect would cause a regression of the student's development. It is therefore the amount of support that is available to the student when these challenges arise that allows for the experience to be positive rather than negative.

The Evolution of Student Development Theory

The theories that exist relative to student development are very much interrelated. That is to say, the major theorists in student development have built on prior conceptualizations of development and change to form their models (see Strange, 1994, for a comprehensive overview of the history of student development theory). For example, Erikson (1959), a student of Freud, was the first to conceptualize life-span development. He believed that individuals move through a chronological series of developmental stages from birth to old age. To progress from one stage to the next, Erikson believed that certain skills or issues had to be resolved, thus resulting in development. It is this stage model that has become the basis for many of the existing theories we have today.

As a case in point, Sanford's work (1962) built on Erikson's thesis (1959), focusing on one particular turning point in the life-span model: that of the college years. His successors then continued to build on this notion, fueled by the changing demographics in the college population and the burgeoning student affairs movement in the United States (Strange, 1994). Throughout the 1960s and 1970s, stage models of development at the college level continued to emerge, including the work of Chickering, McDowell, and Campagna (1969), Kohlberg (1975), and Perry (1968) as well as models that called attention to the social identity of college students such as those by Cass (1979) and Cross (1971). These models, much like Erikson's, focused on a developmental progression through successively more complicated stages in which higher levels of growth marked advancement toward a more self-defined or integrated individual.

Beginning in the 1980s, however, many scholars began to question the notion of the lock-step portrayal of development as well as those theories developed through the predominate study of white affluent males. Theorists such as Gilligan (1978), a student of Kohlberg, and Belenky, Clinchy, Goldberger, and Tarule (1986) also questioned the status quo and contributed new ways of looking at development at the college level and beyond. Contemporary theorists, while building on the earliest works by Piaget (1952), Erikson (1959), and others, continue to introduce new ways of thinking about development and the populations that have not yet been explored in the collegiate years.

Conceptualizing Student Development

Taken together, the historical evolution of developmental theories focusing on the college student population has resulted in several main areas of focus. Traditionally, student development theories have been categorized into several main areas (McEwen, 2005):

Psychosocial development, or the theories concerned with the content of development, including growth or change related to how students view themselves and their abilities, the relationships they have with others in their lives, and the future direction of their lives (Chickering and Reisser, 1993), which encompasses adult development and career development (McEwen, 2005).

Social identity development, or the ways in which "individuals construct their various social identities, namely, race, ethnicity, gender, and sexual orientation" (McEwen, 2005, p. 13).

Cognitive-structural development, which "addresses how students will think about those [psychosocial] issues and what shifts in reasoning will occur" (Knefelkamp, Widick, and Parker, 1978, p. xii). In other words, cognitive-structural theories speak to *how* students think rather than *what* they think (McEwen, 2005). Included in this category are also those theories related to moral and faith development.

Although it is beyond the scope of this monograph to provide an exhaustive overview of all existing theories related to these areas (see Evans, Forney, and Guido-DiBrito, 1998; Knefelkamp, Widick, and Parker, 1978; McEwen, 2005, for a more thorough treatment of student development theory), what follows is a brief overview of each of these theory groups, major theorists within these groups, and then a discussion of their applicability to the doctoral student population.

Psychosocial Development

As discussed, psychosocial theories "examine the content of development, the important issues people face as their lives progress, such as how to define themselves, their relationships with others, and what to do with their lives" (Evans, Forney, and Guido-DiBrito, 1998, p. 32). The developmental tasks or challenges that arise during particular turning points in life are the issues that must be resolved to advance to more complex or higher levels of development. Included under the umbrella of psychosocial development theories are also those related to adult development and career development (discussed below).

The area of student development theory referred to as "psychosocial development" evolved primarily from the work of Erikson (1959), who was one of the first theorists to consider the adult life-span model. His model incorporated growth and change resulting in physical, emotional, and psychological development. Erikson described the life span as occurring in eight development stages or tasks:

Infancy, dealing with a basic task of learning trust and mistrust. The individual requires comfort while also learning to trust others and trust self in the process.

Toddler, focusing on the task of autonomy versus shame and doubt. The individual at this stage seeks to master the physical environment around him or her while acquiring self-esteem.

Preschooler, surrounding issues of initiative versus guilt. At this stage, the individual begins to initiate activities while also developing conscience and sexual identity.

School-age child, tasked with industry and inferiority or trying to develop a sense of individuality and self-worth through the refinement of skills and abilities.

Adolescent, where the individual focuses on task identity versus role confusion. At this stage, the individual works to integrate the many identities he or she has acquired into one larger self-image, despite pressure from peers.

Young adult, wherein the individual struggles between intimacy and isolation. The individual learns at this stage to make a commitment to others such as romantic partners or children.

Middle-age adult, as the individual works to overcome generativity versus stagnation, or the time in which the individual seeks productivity through vocational and life pursuits.

Older adult, in which the individual works to overcome the conflict between integrity and despair. At this final stage of development, the individual reviews his or her life accomplishments, deals with loss of family and friends, and prepares for death.

In this way, Erikson's work (1959) provided the gateway through which contemporary views of psychosocial development emerged, primarily focusing on the adolescent to young adult phases of development of life such as in the college years.

The major theorist known to those familiar with psychosocial development in college students is Chickering and his seven vectors of development. Chickering's early work (Chickering, McDowell, and Campagna, 1969) on college student development became a forerunner of the theory with which we are familiar today. His more recent work with Reisser (1993) focuses on seven vectors of development or "major highways for journeying toward individuation— the discovery and refinement of one's unique way of being—and also communion with other individuals and groups" (p. 35). Although not rigidly sequential, vectors are developmental, building on one another. Specifically, Chickering and Reisser's theory focuses on emotional, interpersonal, and ethical development along with intellectual development. The seven vectors are summarized as follows:

Developing competence, including intellectual competence, physical and manual skills, and interpersonal competence. Intellectual competence includes skills of the mind such as mastering content in a specific subject area as well as critical thinking and reasoning abilities. Physical and manual competence comes through athletic and recreational activities, fitness, and self-discipline; interpersonal competence comes through effective communication skills, leadership skills, and being able to work with others.

Managing emotions, encompassing the ability to handle constructively the myriad emotions in one's life: for example, effectively coping with fears, stresses, and irritations before they become problematic in one's life or relationships as well as balancing selfish needs with the needs of others.

Moving through autonomy toward interdependence, focusing on "freedom from continual and pressing needs for reassurance, affection, or approval from others" (p. 117). This vector also includes a focus on the need for self-direction, problem-solving strategies, and the need to understand and value one's connectedness with others.

Developing mature interpersonal relationships, including tolerance and appreciation of other's differences and building a capacity for intimacy. Skills included in this vector are awareness, respect, openness, curiosity, objectivity, empathy, and altruism.

Establishing identity, building on prior vectors, includes an understanding and acknowledgment of one's personal identity based on gender, ethnic background, and sexual orientation as well as comfort with one's appearance, sense of self in light of feedback from others, and personal stability and integration—in other words, a true sense of self.

Developing purpose, encompassing clear vocational goals, strong commitments to one's interests, and "making and staying with decisions, even in the face of opposition" (Evans, Forney, and Guido-DeBrito, 1998, p. 40).

Developing integrity, or humanizing values, personalizing values, and developing congruence. This vector encompasses the earliest stage when students move from rigid thinking about the world to a more relative view. Personalizing values includes reaffirmation of one's core values and the acknowledgment and respect of other's. Finally, values and actions become congruent, and social responsibility is balanced with self-interest.

Although Chickering and Reisser's conceptualization of psychosocial development (1993) has largely been applied only at the undergraduate level,

Chickering's work has transcended the traditional eighteen- to twenty-two-year-old time frame to consider adult development on a larger scale (Chickering and Havighurst, 1981). As discussed later, psychosocial development is at work throughout all phases of the doctoral student experience, specifically as the student seeks not only to become competent in his or her subject matter but also to establish a professional identity through the attainment of this new degree. Throughout this experience, students also interact with others, and the need for mature relationships and a sense of self in those relationships is vital.

Professional or Career Development

Another aspect of psychosocial development is the development of one's professional identity or "career development." Professional identity development is gained through the process of professional socialization in which an individual learns to adopt the values, skills, attitudes, norms, and knowledge needed for membership in a given society, group, or organization (Merton, 1957).

Socialization typically occurs through two major stages. The initial phase is generally referred to as "anticipatory socialization" and often begins before the individual makes the decision to join the organization as he or she learns about the organization through the recruitment and selection process, aiding the individual in adjusting to the group and becoming assimilated to its norms, values, and attitudes. After successfully gaining entrance to the organization, the individual enters the stage of socialization referred to as "role continuance." This stage consists of the time when the individual experiences the socialization processes that will ultimately influence his or her decision to remain in the organization and to adopt the values, attitudes, and beliefs of the culture (Tierney and Rhoads, 1994).

In the context of graduate school, however, the process of socialization is a bit more complex. Golde (1998) describes graduate school socialization as a process "in which a newcomer is made a member of a community—in the case of graduate students, the community of an academic department in a particular discipline. The socialization of graduate students is an unusual double socialization. New students are simultaneously directly socialized into the role of graduate student and are given preparatory socialization into graduate student life and the future career" (p. 56).

The following chapters discuss socialization theory with respect to doctoral student development, particularly focusing on the student's career development as he or she gains the skills, knowledge, and habits of mind requisite to the degree and the professional field to which he or she aspires.

Adult Development

McEwen (2005) includes adult development as a subsection of psychosocial development, namely because of the nature of adult development theories that conceptualize the life span. In other words, theories of adult development, which focus on life-span and self-concept development, how one deals with particular life events, and the general life course, were inherently a basis for the vectors described by Chickering and Reisser (1993).

While the life-span view of development dates back to the earliest work by Erikson (1959), it is only in the past thirty years that adult development, as a discipline, has emerged. Much like the argument presented in the first chapter surrounding the absence of doctoral students in student development theories, adult development has been conspicuously missing from larger discussions of development because it was traditionally seen as "a barren terrain for development" (Hoare, 2006, p. 4), as development was assumed to stop after adolescence. Recently, however, broader conceptualizations of adulthood and the interrelated focus on adult learning have become more prominent in discussions of development. Adult development is defined as the "systematic, qualitative changes in human abilities and behaviors as a result of interactions between internal and external environments" (p. 8). Much like views of college student development, adult development acknowledges both steps forward and backward in the individual's life, depending on the levels of challenge and support available.

One of the best-known models of adult development is Levinson's (1990). His original work focused primarily on individuals in what he referred to as middle adulthood, between thirty-five and forty-five years of age and centered on the concept of life structure. Specifically, Levinson's work considered the social and physical environment and how these influences affect development in adults. He emphasized six stages of adulthood:

Early adult transition (seventeen to twenty-two years old), encompassing the time when the individual leaves adolescence and begins making the preliminary choices for adult life.

Entering the adult world (twenty-two to twenty-eight years old), including the time during which the individual selects choices related to family, occupation, friendship, lifestyle, and values.

Age 30 transition (twenty-eight to thirty-three years old), during which the individual experiences changes in life structure or may experience a life crisis.

Settling down (thirty-three to forty years old), establishing a niche in society and progressing to the point in which he or she is expected to be more responsible as a parent figure.

Midlife transition (forty to forty-five years old), during which the individual experiences a crisis in respect to the meaning of life and its purpose. This is the point that many refer to as the midlife crisis for men.

Entering middle adulthood (forty-five to fifty years old), including the time when the individual makes new choices, commits to a lifestyle and set of values, and undertakes new tasks.

As many doctoral students enter graduate school at stages two or beyond, this theory is relevant to understanding the tasks that face the student not only in the scope of the doctoral experience but also in life in general.

Encompassed in the concept of adult development is that of adult learning, particularly as learning is of and in itself developmental. Adult learning "is a change in behavior, a gain in knowledge or skills, and an alteration or restructuring of prior knowledge; such learning can also mean a positive change in self-understanding or in the development of personal qualities such as coping mechanisms" (Hoare, 2006, p. 10). In this way, we see the interconnectedness of psychosocial development and adult learning, particularly within the scope of developing competence and establishing identity. They are also vital components of the doctoral experience.

Social Identity Development

Social identity development pertains "to the ways in which individuals construct their various social identities, namely, race, ethnicity, gender, and sexual orientation, and the intersection of these multiple identities" including "social class, ability and disability, and religion" (McEwen, 2005, p. 13). Social identity development shares in common many of the same developmental tasks found in psychosocial development, particularly in Chickering's vector of establishing identity (Chickering, McDowell, and Campagna, 1969); indeed, some scholars have grouped together social identity and psychosocial development in student development theory conceptualizations (Evans, Forney, and Guido-DeBrito, 1998). As a result of the enormous growth of social identity theories, specifically those related to gender, race, ethnicity, and sexual orientation, others such as McEwen (2005) have differentiated this group of theories.

The major theorists included under the umbrella of social identity development include those who began working in the 1970s, characterizing the changing demographic that was emerging in higher education and the desire to better understand nonmajority populations and their personal identities. Although not discussed at length here, one type of social identity development theory is highlighted here to illustrate the dimensions of development that may occur. (Those interested in exploring the other models of social identity development should consult Evans, Forney, and Guido-DiBrito [1998] and Wilson and Wolf-Wendel [2005] for more thorough overviews.)

Racial Identity Development

Helms and Cook (2005) provide an insightful overview of racial and ethnic identity development models, describing racial and ethnic identity development as "the process of development by which individual members of the various socioracial groups overcome the version of internalized racism that typifies their group in order to achieve a self-affirming and realistic racial-group or collective identity" (p. 244). Many models have changed since their inception, but all typically focus on stages or statuses of development in which the individual goes from a racist perspective to one that is more committed and then to an integrated view of race from multiple perspectives. Each stage is gained when the individual is confronted with an issue or event that "shatters an individual's current identity and worldview" (Evans, Forney, and Guido-DeBrito, 1998, p. 74).

Helms and Cook (2005) offer one such model, which they describe as the People of Color Racial Identity Model. This model consists of six stages:

Conformity (preencounter) "involves the person's adaptation and internalization of White society's definitions of one's group(s), either by conforming to the existing stereotypes of one's own group(s) or attempting to become White and assimilated into White culture" (p. 247). Much like other models of racial or ethnic identity development, this stage or status is often the least sophisticated.

Dissonance is characterized "by disorientation, confusion, and unpredictable responses to racial events" (p. 247). Individuals advance to this status after being confronted by an event that challenges their lack of fit in the White world. Much anxiety and consternation is seen at this status.

Immersion "evolves in response to the person's need to replace the group-specific negativity that resides in her or his identity constellation with positive group information" (p. 248). Often seen in this status is the elevation of all things related to the individual's racial group at the exclusion of all others, particularly those things characterized as belonging to the White world.

Emersion is described as "the recognition of the person's need for positive group definition" (p. 249). The individual has positive feelings when surrounded by others who are like him or her and expresses a feeling of joyousness to be in this company.

Internalization includes both a positive commitment to one's own group and a dawning consideration to see positive attributes in other racial or ethnic groups. This status represents a growing ability to use reason and discern positive attributes from many groups.

Integrated awareness is the most sophisticated status. This status involves "the capacity to express a positive racial self and to recognize and resist the multiplicity of practices that exist in one's environment" (p. 249). Individuals who reach this status are able to see the complexity of the surrounding world and to integrate these complex views of race and ethnicity into their own self-concept. Many speak of the "thirst for diversity" as being characteristic of this status.

When considering other aspects of social identity development, we can see the shared traits in Helms and Cook's model (2005) and others, including Cass's model of homosexual identity formation (1979), Phinney's model of ethnic identity development (1989), and Downing and Roush's model of feminist identity development (1985). Taken together, these explanations of social identity development allow for a deeper understanding of how an individual progresses from the least sophisticated view of himself or herself in the world to one that is much more complex—a view that encompasses not only the individual's need for self-identification but also is contextualized in the larger scope of other's needs and identities as well.

Cognitive Development

The theories that pertain to cognitive development arose from the early work of Piaget (1952) and his explorations of intellectual development in children. Since that time, theorists who have focused their research on cognitive development have been concerned with "how people think, reason, and make meaning of their experiences" (Evans, Forney, and Guido-DiBrito, 1998, p. 124). Much like the developmental stages apparent in other theories, cognitive development theories generally encompass stages or positions. Although age is not necessarily tied to a particular stage or position, each stage must be successfully navigated before moving to a higher level of cognitive ability. Akin to the concept of challenge and support (Sanford, 1966), cognitive development occurs through a process of assimilation and accommodation. Assimilation is the "process of integrating new information into existing structures," whereas accommodation is the "process of modifying existing structures or creating new structures to incorporate stimuli that will not fit into existing structures" (Evans, Forney, and Guido-DiBrito, 1998, p. 124). Cognitive development theories have been helpful in understanding how students process information and how they make decisions.

Again, it is beyond the scope of this monograph to offer an exhaustive treatment of all cognitive development models (see Evans, Forney, and Guido-DiBrito, 1998, p. 124; Wilson and Wolf-Wendel, 2005, for more thorough overviews). The following discussion of Perry's theory (1968) is representative of the types of development that may be applicable to doctoral students in their experiences.

Based on Piaget's work (1952), Perry (1968) sought to understand how students make meaning and interpret the learning process. Although criticized for his sole reliance on male students from Harvard as the basis for his theory, Perry's model is nevertheless one of the most referenced and well known of cognitive theories.

Perry's theory (1968) consists of nine static positions, generally described in four main areas: duality, multiplicity, relativism, and commitment. Duality or dualism represents a dichotomous worldview, for example, right and wrong, bad or good. Learning typically occurs as a result of the individual's gaining information or facts from authority figures, that is, the "right" answers from these figures. The transition from dualism occurs when cognitive dissonance arises, in which the individual, for example, may find that an authority figure is incorrect. This transition is what Perry described as disequilibrium.

Multiplicity is a status in which the individual is able to consider multiple or diverse views even while not knowing what is necessarily the "right" answer. In this sense, all views are equally valid in the absence of evidence demonstrating otherwise. Individuals often become much more independent thinkers at this position and may become much more analytically inclined in their thinking (Perry, 1968).

Relativism often occurs as a result of the need to substantiate knowledge. At this point, the individual sees knowledge based more on context and requires evidence to bolster arguments (Perry, 1968).

Commitment results from the integrated knowledge that individuals learn from others as well as their own personal experience and reflection. Part of this commitment is the ability to remain decisive in response to challenges from others (Perry, 1968).

Perry's schema (1968) held tremendous influence for those who followed, including Belenky, Clinchy, Goldberger, and Tarule (1986) in their model of women's ways of knowing and King and Kitchener's reflective judgment model (1994).

Cognitive development in doctoral education is inherently part of the learning process as well as the process required in research, as the student becomes the creator rather than the consumer of knowledge (Katz and Hartnett, 1976). As such, the cognitive development of doctoral students is incorporated into the three phases of development discussed in subsequent chapters.

Conclusion

Student development theories exist to assist professionals, educators, and administrators in better understanding the student populations with whom they work. Although many student development theories were created to explain traditional, eighteen- to twenty-two-year-old college students, many foundational theories were originally taken from the larger psychological literature and work by those such as Piaget, Erikson, Kohlberg, and Perry. In other words, the applicability of these theories to the doctoral student population is apparent and substantiated, as doctoral students are often adults in the context of the learning environment of graduate school.

The three major groups of developmental theories discussed in this chapter—psychosocial, social identity, and cognitive—are also referred to at length in the particular phases of doctoral student development in later chapters. These chapters contextualize the specific dimensions of development in the dynamics of support and challenge that characterize each phase of development in doctoral education. The following chapter, however, focuses on the structure and purpose of doctoral education to inform readers about the scope and nature of the doctoral education experience.

Understanding Doctoral Education

THIS CHAPTER DISCUSSES THE STRUCTURE AND PURPOSES of doctoral education to orient readers to the context and parameters that exist in the doctoral student experience. Specifically, this chapter discusses an overview of doctoral degrees and their purposes, the structure of the doctoral program, today's doctoral students, and key constituencies in the doctoral experience.

Doctoral Degrees and Their Purposes

The Council of Graduate Schools (2005) explains the purpose of the doctoral program as one that prepares "a student to become a scholar: that is, to discover, integrate, and apply knowledge, as well as to communicate and disseminate it" (p. 1). The doctorate can be conceived as the highest academic degree offered in the United States, although several types of doctoral degrees exist. To be exact, twenty-three research doctorate designations are included in the annual Survey of Earned Doctorates (Hoffer and others, 2006). Although this monograph focuses primarily on the Doctor of Philosophy (Ph.D.) degree in the United States, what follows is a brief overview of the three main types of doctoral degrees and the purposes the degrees serve.

Doctoral degrees are divided into three general categories (Hoffer and others, 2006). The first is the professional doctorate or the first professional degree. Individuals who receive this degree generally work in professional fields such as medicine, veterinary medicine, pharmacology, dentistry, psychology, and optometry. Degree designations include M.D., J.D., and Psy.D. These degrees generally do not require a formal academic thesis or dissertation but rather focus on training through lengthy internships and clinical experiences.

The second type of doctoral degree includes those under the umbrella of professional research doctorate such as doctor of education (Ed.D.) and the executive doctorate. Although a thorough discussion of the Ed.D. versus Ph.D. is beyond the scope of this monograph, many institutions offer solely the Ed.D. as the research doctorate in education, while others may offer both, intending the Ed.D. to serve as a professional rather than research degree. As an example, the Ed.D. may include a research component in its training but is equally intended for use in the professional realm (for a discussion of the Ed.D. versus the Ph.D., see Osguthorpe and Wong, 1993; Shulman, Golde, Conklin Bueschel, and Garabedian, 2006; Toma, 2002).

The final type of doctoral degree includes the research doctorate, awarded for academic research in a given field representing original knowledge, typically including the production of a thesis or dissertation demonstrating this research. Although the research doctorate is commonly held to be the Ph.D., other research degrees are also included under this umbrella, including doctor of fine arts (D.F.A.) and the doctor of theology (Th.D.) (Hoffer and others, 2005). The research doctorate is the focus of the remainder of this monograph.

The Structure of the Doctoral Program

The research doctoral program in the United States generally consists of three major components: coursework, examination/assessment of skills gained through coursework, and the production of independent research, often referred to as the thesis or dissertation. The majority of institutions of higher education that offer the research doctorate are those designated as research institutions (formerly designated as Research I institutions) or those whose faculty are highly productive in research, what the Carnegie Foundation for the Advancement of Teaching refers to as doctorate-granting institutions (2007).

Because of differences in disciplines and institutions, the amount of time it may take to complete these three components varies greatly. Doctoral students in education, for example, may focus a majority of their time in coursework, while in the sciences students may take only a few courses and spend their time primarily in research. The three major components and the time it takes to complete them, or what the Council of Graduate Schools (2005) refers to as "time to degree," also vary widely by disciplinary group. Five to six years may be the norm for full-time study in the sciences, but this amount of time generally assumes that the student enters immediately after the baccalaureate. In the humanities and social sciences, full-time study in these programs may entail seven to ten years or more (Bowen and Rudenstine, 1992). In fields like education, however, many students are registered for part-time studies and may enter their programs already with a master's degree in hand. For these students, time-to-degree rates are more difficult to measure but may also last anywhere from seven to ten years or more (Abedi and Benkin, 1987; Council of Graduate Schools, 2008).

Today's Doctoral Students

An overview of the doctoral student population must precede a discussion of doctoral student development. This monograph does not offer an exhaustive discussion of the history of doctoral education (see Berelson, 1960; Gumport, 1993; Malaney, 1988; Nerad, June, and Miller, 1997; Nettles and Millett, 2006; Noble, 1994; Thelin, 2004; Walker and others, 2008, for more thorough treatments of this subject) but rather contextualizes the topic of doctoral student development in the larger scope of the history and evolution of the doctoral student population in the United States.

It is difficult to ascertain the exact numbers of doctoral students throughout the history of doctoral education in the United States, as statistics were not maintained on this population. The data that have been collected are those related to doctoral degree recipients. Although not an accurate measure of the actual enrollment (particularly if we consider attrition rates), doctoral degree recipients nevertheless provide insight into the changing doctoral student population over time, from 1900 to 2000. Where available, this information is presented in Table 1.

The First Doctoral Students (1861–1939)

The first doctoral degrees were awarded in the United States in 1861 at Yale University. The establishment of the Johns Hopkins University, an institution

Table 1
Doctoral Degree Recipients, 1900–2000

Population	1900	1925	1950	1975	2000
Men	94%	83%	91%	78%	57%
Women	6%	17%	9%	22%	43%
American Indian	NA	NA	NA	0.2%	0.7%
Asian/Pacific Islander	NA	NA	NA	1.4%	4.4%
African American	NA	NA	NA	4.2%	5.2%
Latino	NA	NA	NA	1.6%	3.8%
International Students	NA	NA	NA	13% (1964)	31%
Median Age	NA	NA	NA	31.7 years	33.7 years
Students with Disabilities	NA	NA	NA	NA	2%
Married	NA	NA	NA	68.9%	60.5%
First Generation	NA	NA	NA	NA	65%

Source: National Science Foundation, 2006.

dedicated entirely to graduate education, soon followed in 1876 (Walker and others, 2008). Few details are known about the nation's earliest doctoral students, but Thelin (2004) describes these first graduate students as "serious and well prepared" (p. 130) but also few in number. As the idea of graduate education was just beginning to grow in the early 1900s, few stable graduate programs existed (Thelin, 2004). In one of the earliest comprehensive studies on graduate education, John (1934) reported enrollment in the 1870–71 academic year totaling forty-four students among five institutions. The Ph.D. students who did exist worked on specific areas of study under the supervision of faculty members, but as a result of their small numbers and serious nature, these students held marginal roles in the overall campus (Thelin, 2004). It is safe to say, given the college populations of the time, that these first doctoral students represented a demographic that was almost predominately white, affluent, Protestant, and male.

From the late 1800s through the early part of the twentieth century, graduate education continued to grow in the United States, particularly in large public institutions such as those in the Midwest and those established according to the first and second Morrill Acts (Thelin, 2004). The introduction of public historically black colleges and universities through the second Morrill Act, however, did not translate necessarily into more African American doctoral students. Rather, the growth in the number of these students was still contained to private institutions such as Howard University. Doctoral degree attainment by students of color in the United States was slow to develop during the earliest years of graduate education, but by 1939, 119 doctoral degrees had been conferred to African Americans by predominately white institutions (Lucas, 1994).

A Changing Demographic (1940 to the Present)

Graduate education's role in society and higher education grew between the 1940s and the 1960s (Walker and others, 2008). This growth was also evidenced in the changing demographics of the students enrolled. The following sections detail the shifting demographics in doctoral student enrollment throughout the past several decades. Although not an exhaustive treatment of these populations, they nevertheless provide a basis from which to understand the *who* of doctoral student development. Specifically, this brief overview discusses how the doctoral student population has changed in relation to gender, race, national origin, enrollment, age, familial status, educational background, disability, and discipline. Although other subpopulations of doctoral students exist, these demographic characteristics typify the changing doctoral enrollment and those that have received the most attention in the existing literature.

Women. In 1910, women constituted only 10 percent of all doctoral recipients and only 11 percent nearly fifty years later (Berelson, 1960). In fact, more men than women were enrolled in doctoral degree programs until 1987 (National Center for Education Statistics, 2003). Since then, female doctoral enrollment has risen dramatically, with only small increases in male doctoral enrollment. For the first time in 2001–02, more women received doctoral degrees than men in the United States (Wilson, 2004). Today, women doctoral students greatly outnumber men in fields like education and represent 50.8 percent of the overall doctoral student enrollment (Choy and Cataldi, 2006). But although women have made great strides in enrollment in doctoral education, women still are outnumbered in what have been considered traditionally male-oriented fields such as those in the sciences, technology, engineering, and mathematics (STEM) disciplines (National Science Foundation, 2004b). In 2005, for example, the pipeline of women in STEM fields varied greatly, with women earning 62 percent of bachelor's degrees in the biological sciences and 52 percent in chemistry, while men earned 80 percent of bachelor's degrees in engineering and 78 percent in computer science (National Science Board, 2008).

More than any other subpopulation, a substantial amount of research has been conducted on the experience of women in doctoral education. In particular, they have been studied with regard to their relationships with advisors (Clark and Corcoran, 1986; Hartnett, 1981; Heinrich, 1995; Schroeder and Mynatt, 1993), their marginality in underrepresented departments and disciplines (Fox, 2001; Herzig, 2004b; Margolis and Romero, 1998), and their experiences at particular turning points of the doctoral experience in relation to men (Berg and Ferber, 1983; Ellis, 2001; Maher, Ford, and Thompson, 2004; Turner and Thompson, 1993).

Students of Color. As previously stated, the attainment of doctoral degrees by students of color was slow to develop during the earliest years of graduate education (Lucas, 1994). But since the first data were maintained in the late 1930s, enrollment of students of color in graduate programs has increased 167 percent, compared with 13 percent for whites; enrollments among Chicano/Latino students and Asian/Pacific Islanders saw the greatest growth (National Center for Education Statistics, 2003). Although the total number of U.S. citizens earning doctorates has decreased in the last five years, the number of Asian Americans, African Americans, and Chicanos/Latinos earning doctorates has increased, with 40 percent of the doctorates awarded to African American students in education and one of three doctorates awarded to Asian Americans in the life sciences (Hoffer and others, 2004).

Indeed, the years 2004 and 2005 boasted the largest percentage (20 percent) of doctorates ever earned by people of color in the United States (Hoffer and others, 2005, 2006), and in fall 2002 students of color accounted for 27.6 percent of the total doctoral student population (U.S. Department of

Education, 2002). Much like women, however, enrollment in doctoral degree programs for students of color has traditionally been in fields such as education (Hoffer and others, 2006) rather than in many of the STEM fields (National Science Foundation, 2004b).

The research on doctoral students of color and their experiences continues to grow in the literature. Although many early studies group together doctoral students of color in their analyses (Duncan, 1976; Larke, Patitu, Webb-Johnson, and Young-Hawkins, 1999; Nettles, 1990), others have begun to explore the specific experiences of particular populations with regard to their mentoring (Brown, Davis, and McClendon, 1999; Larke, Patitu, Webb-Johnson, and Young-Hawkins, 1999) and their socialization experiences (Castellanos, Gloria, and Kamimura, 2006; Gonzalez, 2006; Green and Scott, 2003; Soto Antony and Taylor, 2004).

International Students. It is beyond the scope of this monograph to speak to the development of international doctoral students, owing to the extreme dearth of research about this population (see Le and Gardner, 2007, for some discussion). Nevertheless, any treatment of doctoral students would be remiss without speaking to this population as a large piece of the changing doctoral student demographic in this country. In the 2003–04 academic year, international student enrollment at the doctoral level represented nearly 20 percent of the total doctoral student population, largely in the STEM fields (Choy and Cataldi, 2006). An awareness of this population and their particular developmental needs and issues must continue to be explored in the literature, as these students keep the United States competitive in the domestic and global economy, research, and innovation and are essential to U.S. foreign affairs (Sodowsky and others, 1994).

Part-Time Students. Much like that for international students, any discussion of doctoral student demographics in the United States would be incomplete without an understanding of the changing enrollment patterns that have been witnessed among this population. Doctoral education has seen a tremendous growth in the number of part-time students enrolling. In total doctoral student enrollment in the 2003–04 academic year, only 50.3 percent of all students were enrolled full time. In fields other than those in education (where only 24.1 percent of students are full time), full-time doctoral students represented only 53.8 percent (Brown, 2005; Syverson, 1999). Even though this population continues to grow, the research is nevertheless sparse about part-time doctoral students and their experience in graduate school.

Older Students. A nontraditional student in doctoral education could be considered a student who is older than the typical twenty-two- to thirty-year-old age range for undergraduates. These students, unlike their "traditional" counterparts, may not come directly to graduate school after graduating with a bachelor's degree and may instead work for many years or may choose other pathways before deciding to matriculate. In 2004, the median age of those earning a doctorate was 33.3 years (Hoffer and others, 2005), but like most topics in graduate education, age varies widely by disciplinary context. For example, those in the STEM fields typically earn their degrees in their early thirties (31.7 years was the median in 2004), in the humanities in their midthirties (35.0 years median), in education in their midforties (43.1 years median), and in other professional fields in their late thirties (37.0 years median) (Hoffer and others, 2006). Therefore, what is considered an older student in each of these disciplinary contexts also varies widely, but the experience of those who are outliers with regard to their age is often different from those in the typical age range of doctoral students in their fields.

Much like other underrepresented populations, very little research has been conducted on the experiences of older doctoral students, and the research that is completed is disparate and related to particular issues or concerns of the older population (Barker, Felstehausen, Couch, and Henry, 1997; Gardner, 2008b; Lenz, 1997).

Students with Families. In 1960, Berelson commented on a new change among the graduate student population in the United States: students who were married and had children. He stated that this shift "has changed the whole environment of graduate study" (p. 134), as these students "have families to be dedicated to as well as their studies, and some deans feel that this has had a big and undesirable effect on graduate work in distracting the students' attention from what should be intensive devotion to a subject" (p. 135).

The number of graduate students with children has changed dramatically since 1957, given the fact that the Survey of Earned Doctorates (Hoffer and others, 2005) reported nearly 60 percent of 2004 doctoral recipients as married, with nearly another 6 percent in a marriage-like relationship. The majority of married or partnered students graduated in 2004 with degrees in the physical and life sciences as well as other STEM-related fields (Hoffer and others, 2005).

Recently, more research has been conducted on students with families as well as married students. One study in particular found that married students were more likely to complete their programs than single students (Price, 2006). Although these concerns certainly arise in the existing research on doctoral education (Berelson, 1960; Gardner, 2008b; Nettles and Millett, 2006), more research must be conducted to examine their particular concerns and obstacles in the doctoral process.

First-Generation Students. Yet another growing and changing demographic in doctoral education is the increasing number of first-generation students. First-generation status has been referred to often in the literature on undergraduate students but is rarely discussed with regard to graduate or doctoral students (an article by Kniffin [2007], offers some treatment of the subject). First-generation status can be conceptualized in multiple ways, but, for the purposes of our discussion, it refers to students' parents having not received any higher education degree (Hoffer and others, 2002). In 2004, more than one-third of all doctorates granted were to those who reported first-generation status, with neither of their parents having earned a bachelor's degree, much less an advanced graduate degree. The percentages of first-generation students among underrepresented students are even higher, with more African American, Latino, and Native American graduates being first generation than their white counterparts (Hoffer and others, 2005). Much like part-time enrollment status, first-generation status in graduate school varies widely by disciplinary context, with more students in education reporting first-generation status than students in the humanities and STEM fields (Hoffer and others, 2005; Nettles and Millett, 2006).

Students with Disabilities. If little research exists about other underrepresented populations' experiences while in graduate school, the research on doctoral students with disabilities is by far the sparsest. Nevertheless, students with disabilities constituted 1.5 percent of all those earning the doctorate in 2004 (Hoffer and others, 2005)—or 634 individuals. Physical or orthopedic disabilities were reported most often, followed by learning disabilities. Students with disabilities were more likely in 2004 to have elected degrees in non-STEM fields, while more women than men reported having a disability. Although students with disabilities are reported to have lower completion rates and longer time-to-degree rates at the undergraduate level, at the graduate level these students enroll at rates similar to those students without reported disabilities (U.S. Department of Education and National Center for Education Statistics, 1999).

Disciplinary Differences. Finally, to best understand doctoral students, it is vital to understand the differences they experience related to discipline. Unlike undergraduate education, which is generally studied monolithically, doctoral education must be understood through the disciplinary lens in which it is situated (Golde, 2005). And although it is impossible to discuss the hundreds of different disciplines that offer doctoral degrees in this country, the caveat must nevertheless be offered that difference certainly does exist. Disciplines have their own particular qualities, cultures, codes of conduct, values, and distinctive intellectual tasks (Becher, 1981; Biglan, 1973; Clark, 1987) that ultimately influence the experiences of the faculty, staff, and most especially the students. Furthermore, the paradigmatic assumptions that exist in particular disciplines (Biglan, 1973; Braxton and Hargens, 1996) may also play a role in a student's exposure to developmental opportunities.

For example, students in the sciences tend to choose advisors or research directors very early in their programs and subsequently begin work on their dissertation research very early as well. Stable funding is also generally provided for the doctoral student in the sciences, and much of the research done is completed in teams (Golde, 1998). On the opposite end of the disciplinary continuum are the humanities, which are organized more around coursework that focuses on a broad area of knowledge. Instead of working directly in the research enterprise, financially supported humanities students spend more of their time as teaching assistants. These students generally do not make a significant connection with the advisor until later in the program, often only after completing the qualifying examination process. When the student begins the research endeavor, it is generally completed in isolation (Katz and Hartnett, 1976; Walker and others, 2008). Doctoral students in education are typically part time and unfunded, have programs strongly focused on coursework, and work independently on dissertations that may be oriented more toward their full-time professional roles (Walker and others, 2008).

Key Constituencies in the Doctoral Program

Several other key individuals greatly influence the doctoral student experience. Graduate faculty members who serve as the students' instructors in their courses and become the students' dissertation committee members, assistant-ship supervisors, committee chairs or advisors, and mentors play a large and often pivotal role in the doctoral student experience. Faculty members also guide doctoral students through the socialization process and assist them in obtaining careers after graduation (Council of Graduate Schools, 1995).

Similarly, graduate program administrators, graduate school administrators, and support staff play important roles in the doctoral student experience, as these individuals provide guidance and assistance through programmatic and bureaucratic structures that are an inherent part of the graduate school experience (Council of Graduate Schools, 2005).

In addition, doctoral students interact very often with their graduate student peers, working together in research labs, sharing office space, and teaching—and most definitely in their class work. Doctoral students' peers in their program also play a vital role in the doctoral student experience, as these individuals often serve as informal mentors, advisors, and supportive colleagues throughout the doctoral program (Gardner, 2007).

Depending on the students' enrollment status and discipline, they may also be engaged in other types of opportunities that will greatly influence their experiences. Full-time students may receive funding through fellowships or assistantships that support their education, provide a meager stipend, and perhaps pay for insurance benefits. Assistantship opportunities such as for those engaged in research, teaching, or university staff generally consist of a twenty-hour-per-week commitment. In these experiences, students interact with their supervisors, peers, colleagues, and other university employees. This experience, including the skills gained and the relationships formed, also plays an important role in the doctoral program (Ethington and Pisani, 1993; Nyquist and Wulff, 1996).

For those doctoral students who work full time outside their graduate programs, the relationships they have with existing colleagues and workplaces are also important components of the students' experiences. Students who work may have to learn how to balance the role of student with the role of professional, with often competing demands on their time and energies (Davis and McCuen, 1995; Gardner, 2008b).

Finally, it is also important to discuss the other important players in a doctoral student's experience: those outside the graduate program. Family members, partners, children, and friends all serve vital roles in the doctoral student's experience. Balancing these relationships with graduate work is often tenuous, particularly for those students who are also parents of small children, are involved in serious relationships, and have family care responsibilities (Gardner, 2008b).

Taken together, the structure of and the players involved in the doctoral program are key to understanding the developmental nature of the doctoral experience. The next chapters begin a thorough discussion of development in the three phases of the doctoral experience. In each chapter, quotations from interviews with 177 doctoral students are included to highlight the developmental challenges and sources of support that characterize each phase.

Phase I: Entry

I don't think I would have known exactly what to expect before I got here. I think that is the case for a lot of people going to graduate school; they don't know the questions to ask and they don't really know what to expect and sometimes they're disappointed.

History student

When I moved here I didn't know anybody, no one. No family, no nothing. And so the graduate students here in the department became my friends and now they're my best friends—all the people in the department.

Chemistry student

THE EXPERIENCE OF DOCTORAL EDUCATION does not begin on the first day of class; rather, it begins long before the student even applies to the program. In what is generally referred to as "anticipatory socialization" (Lovitts, 2001; Weidman, Twale, and Stein, 2001), the individual develops understandings of the doctoral experience from sources ranging anywhere from his or her own undergraduate or master's degree experiences, departmental Web sites, conversations with peers, and even the media. The understandings that students glean from these experiences result in the knowledge and attitudes that students bring with them during their first days and months of the graduate program, or what is referred to as "Phase I." Phase I encapsulates the time leading up to and continuing through the first year of the doctoral program.

This chapter begins the discussion of doctoral student development in the context of the three phases of the developmental model. It covers the particular challenges and sources of support for doctoral students in Phase I: admission, orientation, coursework, initial relationships with peers and faculty, changes in how the student thinks and understands knowledge, the transition from undergraduate to graduate school expectations, and departure of students that results from a lack of support during these challenges. The remaining sections of this chapter specifically address each of these major developmental tasks and challenges facing the doctoral student in this phase and the corresponding types of support available to the student to mitigate these challenges. Integrated in each of these challenges is the existing literature related to development and doctoral education that further explains the tasks in the phase.

Challenge: The Initial Transition

As a new student it's intimidating because there's all this new information.

Communications student

The first year was one of the toughest years of my life, I think.

Math student

It was a very difficult transition for me because I had never lived on my own and had never moved to another state or moved away from my parents. I was away from family support, away from my friends, starting school, and I hadn't been in school for three years so just getting back into being a student again and not having that emotional support.

Psychology student

As the above three quotes demonstrate, the initial transition to the doctoral program can be both an exciting and difficult time for students. For those who leave home and the support of friends and family to move to a new location and even perhaps a new culture, the experience can be doubly intimidating. Indeed, the transition to doctoral education begins the first of what will become a series of transitions in the doctoral student's experience. Schlossberg, one of the best-known theorists on the topic of transitions in adulthood, defines a transition as "any event or non-event that results in changed relationships, routines, assumptions, and roles" (Goodman, Schlossberg, and Anderson, 2006, p. 33). According to these authors, transitions are in and of themselves developmental, particularly the psychosocial development that occurs as a result of the transition in which individuals begin to understand themselves and the world around them differently in relation to the context and outcome of the transition.

Moreover, the developmental nature of transition theory is evidenced through its prescribed stages of moving in, moving out, and moving through the transition. The first stage involves moving in or out of the new situation, and once in this new situation, adults must learn how to "balance their activities with other parts of their lives and how to feel supported and challenged during their journey" (Goodman, Schlossberg, and Anderson, 2006, p. 49). When viewing this model of transition, one can clearly see the connections between this model and that of socialization, in which the individual must "learn the ropes" of the new environment or culture (Van Maanen, 1984). The following quotation by a doctoral student in communications illustrates these changes and transitions: "I was terrified. I was so scared. I felt like a fish out of water because you know I was coming from a very different school. There was a period of adjustment and then learning the language of the department so that was a little unnerving."

When seen in the context of the new doctoral student's transition to the new environment of graduate school, the student experiences new roles, relationships, routines, and assumptions about life and others as well as adjusts to what Goodman, Schlossberg, and Anderson (2006) refer to as "hang-over identity" (p. 50). Hang-over identity describes the tendency to "hang on" to a role from a previous environment, for example, someone who is retiring and having a difficult time transitioning away from the identity that was encompassed in that position. For many doctoral students, particularly those who may be in transition from a full-time professional role to that of a full-time student role, this concept of "hang-over identity" is particularly poignant (Gardner and McCoy, 2008).

Students enter their doctoral programs, however, with both enthusiasm and trepidation. These feelings of expectation and uncertainty are often bolstered by their anticipatory socialization. As previously mentioned, students may receive some of their anticipatory socialization from prior academic experiences in undergraduate programs, perhaps through observing doctoral students in their departments, or through work on the master's degree. Students who attend private liberal arts institutions, however, may not have this exposure to graduate education other than through what they have heard from peers, from faculty, or even what they see in media representations (Lovitts, 2001). Regardless, most students may not be ready for what they will experience upon entering their doctoral programs (Gardner, 2007; Lovitts, 2001). For example, one student in chemistry stated:

> *I think in a lot of ways I wasn't really fully prepared. I mean, I had an intellectual understanding of say, the credit requirements, I knew what courses were available, I knew what I would need to take, I knew the sort of strict on-paper requirements of what I would need to do in order to earn a degree, but the intangibles—what the culture would be like, how graduate education is run, how it's different from undergraduate education—I don't think I was really prepared for that and I didn't think that I really could be unless I actually experienced it.*

Support: Orientation

One of the things that I learned about a Ph.D. program is that it is nothing like a master's program. I think I was a little—I would not use the word 'arrogant'—confident that because I had been through an honors program, been through a rigorous master's program, that I could then, you know, not that it would be easy, but I felt I was really grounded in what I was doing. And then I realized that I wasn't. I felt that I was so far behind all of the other people.

English student

You don't retain 70 percent of the stuff that you learn [in orientation]. You're handed a million pieces of paper that you're never going to look at again. It didn't really help. Did it prepare me for what was about to happen? No.

History student

One of the first formal programmatic experiences a doctoral student encounters may be orientation. Orientation programs in graduate education are often quite different from their undergraduate counterparts. Whereas undergraduate orientation programs have grown to be multiday or even multiweek events that engage parents and families and speak to the holistic nature of the undergraduate experience (Pascarella and Terenzini, 2005), graduate orientation programs are often much less comprehensive. And, although a growing body of literature examines the importance of orientation for graduate students (Barker, Felstehausen, Couch, and Henry, 1997; Forney and Davis, 2002; Owen, 1999; Rosenblatt and Christensen, 1993; Taub and Komives, 1998; Vickio and Tack, 1989; Vlisides and Eddy, 1993), the effects of this experience on student development are largely unexamined. In fact, even the Council of Graduate School's documentation (2004) offers only a perfunctory nod to orientation at the graduate level. What is known, however, is that about 30 to 40 percent of the attrition that occurs in doctoral education happens during the first year (Bowen and Rudenstine, 1992; Golde, 1998; Lott and Gardner, forthcoming), necessitating a better understanding of this transition.

In the context of the transition the student experiences, Goodman, Schlossberg, and Anderson (2006) explain the necessity of orientation: "Institutions need to devote a great deal of time to orientation, a process designed to help individuals know what is expected of them" (p. 49). These expectations are what students often share as being the most ambiguous part of their initial experience in their doctoral programs (Gardner, 2007). Lovitts (2001) found that a large part of the attrition that occurred in the initial stages of the doctoral program could have been prevented if the structure of the program had been different.

According to Vickio and Tack (1989), a comprehensive graduate orientation can assist in alleviating students' concerns and fears, provide direction about new academic demands, and establish new relationships. Moreover, they point out, graduate student orientation can go a long way in introducing the student to the departmental policies and structures as well as the larger university level of expectations and services. In this way, the student is then being socialized to the department, the discipline, and the larger environmental context of the institution while also being given the opportunity to begin forming initial relationships with peers and faculty. This type of orientation or introduction will assist students in becoming more integrated into these environments, thereby facilitating retention (Tinto, 1993). Much like undergraduate and first-year orientation programs have been shown to be beneficial to student satisfaction and retention, graduate student orientation may also assist students in feeling they belong and can be successful in this new environment, a key aspect of psychosocial development (Chickering and Reisser, 1993).

Understanding the developmental nature of the doctoral experience also assists in creating a developmentally appropriate orientation program. As the history student's quote above illustrates, many orientation programs unleash mountains of paperwork on students—overwhelming the student with details only to be forgotten later—rather than constructing orientation or induction programs that assist the student by explaining immediate concerns or needs (Where is the library? Where do I park? What classes do I need to take? Who are my peers and faculty members?). Providing students with comprehensive handbooks and Web sites at orientation may meet the needs of the program and graduate school that want students to be aware of structures and guidelines but allow students to access them as needed throughout the program (Gardner, 2007). Subsequent sessions that provide details at turning points such as those arranged by the three phases of the conceptual framework may therefore not only be more successful in reaching students but also allow them to seek out information valuable to them at a particular time.

Challenge: Coursework

My undergraduate experience was immensely different from my graduate experience. My major was very factual, not much thinking. Well, there was a lot of thinking involved, but it was a lot of laws—there was no theory, it was law, it was chemistry. I liked the type of education where you could stretch the limits and you could have a personal style. So grad school is like a degree full of ambiguity, almost. There is no law of human behavior, so it just totally threw me into this new realm of thinking where anything is possible. It really challenges my thought process. It really challenges me to think creatively and try different things. It's like a puzzle and there's no answer and you have to try to find the best answer.

Higher education student

In the first days of the program, students also attempt to make meaning of the explicit and implicit expectations faculty members express in their coursework. Accordingly, students work diligently to prove to themselves, their peers, and their professors that they are capable and worthy to be a part of the intellectual community of graduate school and their disciplinary fields (Katz, 1976). Much of the development that students undergo in this right can be conceptualized as psychosocial development.

Using Chickering and Reisser's work (1993) as a model, we can easily see the psychosocial development that may occur as a result of the early coursework experiences at the doctoral level. Consider the following quotes from several students: "I learned how to write better, connect my ideas, organize my ideas better. I learned how to read, not faster, but I don't know, I can understand things if I read now—I don't have to go back and read it a second time. And I'm more vocal now" [Li]. "The only thing I had to focus on [when an undergrad] was school and now as a Ph.D. student and working full time and married, there [are] other time pressures that I deal with now that I didn't have to deal with then" [Brent]. "When I got to graduate school, [I had] a lack of self-confidence, [I was] very intimidated, very quiet. I think my professors would now be shocked how quiet I was because I didn't say anything. I took extra long writing papers. I was so vulnerable; if they said anything that would impact my confidence or that I was not adequate enough to perform at that level of graduate student, my path would have unraveled" [James]. "I saw myself moving from feeling like you're just a student, you're just in school, to thinking about it in terms of a career" [Donna].

In each of these examples, we see evidence of Chickering's seven vectors. Li is concerned about developing and demonstrating skills required to be successful in her doctoral program (Achieving Competence), Brent is learning to balance his independence with other mature relationships in his life (Developing Mature Relationships), James has grown in his self-confidence and self-esteem through his doctoral experience (Establishing Identity), and Donna is considering her identity with respect to her future career (Developing Purpose). These students are all experiencing development in the context of their own identities and in relation to those around them.

A related challenge occurring in the first few months of the student's coursework is learning to manage the workload of graduate school. One mathematics student shared, "Starting here was really hard. When I was in college I was just kind of coasting and didn't really need a lot of effort. But here they put me in three advanced classes right away and I needed to study all the time." Similarly, a student in higher education expressed, "I don't think I was prepared for the pace. I always tell my family or friends who haven't gone to this level is that what makes it difficult is the pace and the amount of work we have to do in a very specific time. I wasn't prepared for that pace. Every minute counted; you had to prioritize." For many students, the amount of work required to be successful in their classes and the increased amount of energy required to succeed is something altogether new for them. In this way, students begin questioning their ability and their competency, again related to Chickering and Reisser's first vector of achieving competence (1993).

In addition, many students talk about the need to find balance among academic responsibilities, work duties, and personal relationships. For part-time students and students with children and mature relationships, finding this balance may be even more difficult (Gardner, 2007). One communications student said, "Balancing the amount of time that I have to spend on my academic work—that's the biggest struggle and making sure that I'm a good father," whereas an English student shared, "I did not yet know how to balance it all but I think it's the nature of graduate school. You're assigned more than you can physically do so it becomes sort of the art of prioritizing. Figuring out, okay, what is relevant to my interests? What is relevant to the coursework? What can be skimmed and what needs more attention? You just have to prioritize." A chemistry student, however, talked about the negative effect that graduate school life may have on relationships: "If you're going to be a married student coming into graduate school or if you have a relationship and you're coming into graduate school, you need to be aware of the fact that it's going to take a toll on your relationship. You could come out better and stronger for it or it could have very negative effects on your relationship because it is so time consuming and emotionally consuming. You need to understand as a student coming in that it's going to affect your personal life in a way that I think, well, that you don't expect it to."

From the perspective of student development, learning to balance one's life commitments and responsibilities is an inherent part of what Levinson (1990) discussed in his conceptualization of early adulthood. Moreover, the prioritization of one's interests with one's commitments is a part of Chickering and Reisser's seven vectors (1993), allowing the student to develop purpose and move from autonomy toward interdependence.

Challenge: Changes in Thinking

I truly wasn't prepared for the type of studying that I would have to do. A lot less repetition, a lot more discussion with my peers, which is amazingly different [from] what I had before when you listened to the teacher, you write it down, you hand it in, and then you get it back. There was not much discussion in the class, a lot of big 'A' authority teaching: You're going to listen to me and I'm going to learn this. Whereas in grad school, I wasn't really ready for that interaction, so it took me a while to really read and come prepared to class to share my opinions of the readings—and I could have an opinion of the readings—it wasn't the end all be all.

Higher education student

As this quote illustrates, doctoral students are not just learning how to think differently in their coursework but also how to see themselves differently with regard to knowledge. Accordingly, doctoral students also begin to develop a changing view of themselves in relation to their faculty members, seeing themselves increasingly as those who can also create and disseminate knowledge, a key component of cognitive development (Pascarella and Terenzini, 2005).

Many students talk about this transition from rote learning to a more active, productive role in the knowledge process (Gardner, 2008c). For example, one higher education student shared:

> *I think you are absolutely more connected to school and the ideas [in grad school]. I think when you're an undergrad, you're just trying to get done. When you are a grad student, you are looking at the concepts and ideas on a deeper level. I think you are actually trying to learn for the sake of learning. As an undergrad, I just felt like I was trying to get done, to get a degree, to get a job. And I think in graduate school it's one of the only times in your life you get a chance to think about things at a different level than you have in the past.*

A chemistry student remarked, "It's not necessarily the coursework—it's more about how you think about things."

One of the few scholars who has addressed this area is Baxter Magolda (1996, 1998), who examined the epistemological development and self-authorship of graduate students at the master's degree level. Research related to epistemological development, or development in relation to understanding the nature of knowledge, has been applied by many at the undergraduate level (Baxter Magolda, 1995; Belenky, Clinchy, Goldberger, and Tarule, 1986; Perry, 1968) but is relatively absent from the existing literature about graduate students. It is only perhaps through an examination of the adult development literature that we are able to surmise the dynamics of cognitive and epistemological development that occurs at this level.

Weathersby (1981) refers to what doctoral students experience in her model of ego development: "Ego development is an implicit aim of higher education and can be one of its most significant results. Stages of ego development constitute qualitatively different frames of reference for perceiving and responding to experience. Each successive stage represents a major reorganization of ways of understanding and reacting to situations, people, and ideas—a watershed change in patterns of thinking and feeling about oneself, others, authority, ethics, knowledge, and the central concerns that hold a life together" (p. 51). In other words, her view of the type of development that students experience at this level encompasses much more than solely cognitive development but rather interpersonal and psychosocial development as well.

Learning like this stands in close relation to what Lave and Wenger (1991) refer to as "situated learning." Much like other scholars of adult development who see learning as an event deeply rooted in social interaction (Merriam and Clark, 2006; Tennant and Pogson, 2002). Lave and Wenger describe learning as "an integral and inseparable aspect of social practice" (p. 31). This conceptualization is easily applied to the doctoral student experience in which students may learn together in seminar-type coursework, in laboratory settings, or in study groups, learning together or learning in close association with a faculty member (or master) in an apprenticeship style. In this context, therefore, socialization and learning unite in a community of learners.

In these communities of learners, doctoral students also seek experiences that verify their experiences and incorporate their learning needs, which are key tenets of adult learning. Adult learning is built on three assumptions: (1) acknowledging the experience of learners, (2) establishing an adult teacher-learner relationship, and (3) promoting autonomy and self-direction (Tennant and Pogson, 2002, p. 9). Students often talk about the shift in their experiences from undergraduate to graduate school and the excitement they feel about this change: "I absolutely love graduate school more than undergraduate just based on the fact that I came to class having something to contribute, and what I have to say is valuable and encouraged. Learning [in graduate school] was galvanized because in undergraduate it wasn't like that—we would just sit there and if we didn't speak the professor could[n't] care less." Or according to a higher education student, "I get a chance to express myself more and to be involved in class discussion, and they [professors and classmates] actually want to know what I think about certain things. In undergrad I kind of missed that—they just put knowledge in my head without asking me."

Seminar-format classes often contribute to these fundamentals of adult learning, allowing the student to be a vital part of the class's content, connecting the student to the faculty member, and allowing for student independence in learning. Moreover, these tenets of adult learning contribute to the larger goals of the doctoral program, as they allow students to transition to the role of independent researcher, allowing for their experience and their self-direction to propel them to the status of colleague in the profession.

Students may also experience social identity development in the context of their coursework. Although this experience may not be universal, learning opportunities that allow students to question epistemological differences may go far in this regard. An example illustrates this point: Janet began her doctoral program in cultural studies last year. Before her enrollment in graduate school, she received a master's degree in business administration and worked for several years in a bank. During her undergraduate years, however, she found herself drawn to the topics discussed in her general studies courses such as issues related to sociological differences like race and gender. After talking to a few friends in the past several years with degrees in cultural studies, she decided to pursue her doctorate in this field, as she feels this is where her true passions lie.

Upon entering the program and beginning her coursework, Janet began to have second thoughts. Many of the readings she was asked to consider in her first few classes challenged the worldview she had maintained throughout her entire life. Discussions of privilege in particular were the most upsetting to Janet, and she often left classes with a headache.

As the semesters progressed, Janet began to see her field and her own life in a different light. Although it was not an easy time for Janet in regard to the paradigmatic shift she has had to experience, she feels that she has grown as a human being and that she will be better able not only to manage her upcoming research but also to relate to others in her community and in the world.

Janet is a composite of many students who, more often than not, are in disciplines that require them to examine sociopolitical assumptions and theories regarding the nature of knowledge and truth such as those in the social sciences. Students in these kinds of disciplines have shared that these experiences make an enormous impression on their identities and how they view themselves in the larger global context. Two examples from students at two different institutions illustrate these changes: "[My class work] really prompted me to just question my life and my own education, my own background, and my community, and society in general, and the world. It just takes somebody to just open your eyes. It's not the world has changed, it's just that my eyes have changed." "[A course on diversity issues] totally changed the way I look at everything from small things to big things. As I'm aware of certain things, I'm also aware that nobody else is aware of it so I feel so out of place when I go someplace and I recognize certain things but to everyone else that's normal. When I say something, they'll say, 'Where's she coming from?' It's an eye opener."

In this context, students experience psychosocial development with respect to how they see others and are more open to other ways of being, but they also experience social identity development with regard to how they see themselves in terms of race, gender, sexual orientation, and other sociocultural identities.

Although these early coursework experiences can be positive for students, other early experiences can be negative with regard to students' social identity development. For example, many students of color and women may enter into fields where they are generally underrepresented (Ellis, 2001). Having to frequently represent "the minority" viewpoint in coursework or feelings of isolation can lead to dissatisfaction and questions about retention for some students (Gay, 2004). Moreover, early negative interactions with peers and faculty members may exacerbate a feeling of not belonging among these students and may cause them to question their place in the doctoral program. One female student of color in chemistry shared, "I think my first year was definitely the worst year that I've had. It was a big transition for me because I'm a nontraditional student [in age], and I studied undergrad at a very, very small liberal arts women's college. It was very much a wonderful, rich learning environment for me. When I came here it was just horrible. It was extremely competitive. A lot of gender issues, especially, you know, because I'm a woman working in chemistry. It's a heavily male-dominated field and just a lot of sexist attitudes. It was a really horrid experience for me."

Challenge: The Transition from Undergraduate to Graduate School Expectations

Graduate school is a totally different experience from undergrad and I think a lot of people don't realize that. Graduate school, the way I see it, is what you make of it. Most individuals in graduate school are there because they want to be there or because they need to be there for professional opportunities—you can't say that for undergrads. Undergrads have different reasons for being there—they want to party, mom and dad are making them go to college so they don't have to work, their motives are different. I think in graduate school that development, because you're intrinsically motivated, has to be something within the person and then you take it to the next level.

Higher education student

An overarching aspect of this first phase is the transition the student experiences from undergraduate to graduate school expectations. As previously stated, transitions are an important part of adult development and encompass changes from one role to another (Goodman, Schlossberg, and Anderson, 2006). Inherent in many of the other aspects of Phase I delineated above, this transition is essential to the student's future success and persistence in the rest of the doctoral program.

This transition is not only in relation to coursework and faculty relationships but also in regard to the student's view of the educational process. Specifically, students begin to see the more independent and self-directed nature of graduate education when compared with the more regimented and proscribed undergraduate program (Gardner, 2008c; Lovitts, 2005). As mentioned earlier, self-directed learning is a vital component of adult learning and adult development (Merriam and Clark, 2006). Self-directed learning focuses on facilitating students to become autonomous and self-directed in their learning and educational pursuits, a key part of the doctoral experience. An oceanography student summed it up well: "It's more independent. Seems like each degree you move up is a lot more independent than the last." A psychology student underscored the independent nature of the doctoral experience: "When you get to this point and level of education, there's nobody there to hold your hand or push you. You really have to want to do this." In this way, the independent nature of doctoral education requires students to develop further in terms of their psychosocial development (Chickering and Reisser, 1993), particularly relating to the development of competence and self-identity as a burgeoning scholar.

Inherent in the more independent nature of doctoral education is the amount of ambiguity that students face as graduate students compared with their undergraduate experiences (Gardner, 2008c). Although the undergraduate experience is much more concrete—involving choosing a major, fulfilling particular requirements, and graduating, graduate education is much more loosely structured. One English student related, "[Starting my program] was really tough for me because there was no set of concrete rules. Everybody had their own set of rules and you're just not aware of what they are," while an oceanography student remarked, "I was just sort of floating around; I really didn't know what to do." These examples demonstrate that students are learning to think for themselves and find self-direction and motivation, a key part of the cognitive development in Perry's scheme (1968). At the same time, students are developing psychosocially with regard to developing purpose (Chickering and Reisser, 1993), as they must decide on their own course in life and remain committed to it even in the absence of direction from others.

An additional source of ambiguity for doctoral students in Phase I may result from a new professional identity that many full-time students acquire, that of graduate assistant. Assistantships at the graduate level can vary greatly from teaching assistant, staff assistant, or even research assistant (Nyquist and Wulff, 1996), but all require advanced skills and a new professional personality that many students may not have experienced before. This being said, the student may be learning to balance his or her assistantship duties with coursework as well as mastering the skills and requirements the assistantship demands. As many students in the sciences, for example, may be working in labs with their faculty advisors, the student-faculty relationship may be different from those they have had in the past, requiring psychosocial development on their part in relation to managing emotions, developing mature relationships, and demonstrating their competencies (Chickering and Reisser, 1993).

Support: Initial Relationships with Peers and Faculty

I would say that my fellow graduate students were probably the most helpful resource. I think that especially the first year, when it was so disorienting, having a group of people that had been here already and sort of knew the ropes a little bit better was critical in helping make it easier to get into this whole process.

History student

Professors are people. You know, as an undergrad, there's a different type of relationship. [In] grad school, as a doctoral student or a doctoral candidate, it becomes more of a collaborative effort.

Higher education student

Although faced with many challenges in Phase I, the support offered to doctoral students at this early time can facilitate the development that occurs. In this context, inherent psychosocial development occurs in relation to developing mature interpersonal relationships but, for many students, a layer of professional development as well. Support from relationships with peers and faculty members is discussed below.

Peer Relationships

In the first days and months of the doctoral program, students may seek a sense of belonging and integration (Tinto, 1993), generally consisting of relationships with peers. A mathematics student shared, "The first transition period it was kind of scary and kind of lonely and everything because I didn't know people," or another, who remarked, "That was really important to me, right away, to have a sort of, you know, a group. Immediately when we started class we all started working together and made a lot of friends." In concert with the cognitive development occurring in the coursework, students may also gain much from these peer relationships. A higher education student remarked, "I think I learn a lot from my peers. I've had peer mentoring for the last two semesters and it helped me tremendously with my class work. Some people took me under their wing and that helps a lot. Peer mentoring is totally different [from] what your professors can do for you because your peers are kind of on the same level and they are doing it so they know and understand it better." In this case, the relationships these students form with more advanced peers become a form of socialization in and of itself (Gardner, 2007, 2008c; Lovitts, 2001), preparing the student to take on more advanced roles and more advanced knowledge and skills in future phases.

These supportive peer relationships are also more readily attainable for many Phase I students who may be initially intimidated by faculty. One chemistry student stated about his peers, "They're at the same level you are, they've experienced some of the things that you're experiencing now, or they've experienced it before so they can tell you what to expect and you can interact with them. There's not that social distance that exists initially between graduate students and faculty members because of the difference in status. I immediately fell upon other graduate students as a sort of support group." Indeed, the difference in relationships may be characteristic of the shifting understandings these students are beginning to experience with respect to their role as graduate students as well as their role in relation to authority, something discussed in many of the major cognitive and moral development theories. In particular, students may begin making a shift from seeing the older faculty member as the source of knowledge and authority to seeing themselves as capable of producing and evaluating knowledge as well. The power shift from authority figure to self is part of the student's moral development and self-concept (Belenky, Clinchy, Goldberger, and Tarule, 1986; Kohlberg, 1975; Perry, 1968).

Faculty Relationships

As important as peer relationships are to doctoral students, many students choose their graduate programs on the basis of the faculty members with whom they will work (Council of Graduate Schools, 2005). These faculty relationships over time contribute immensely to the student's learning and success in both graduate school and their future profession (Clark and Corcoran, 1986). Through the mechanism of socialization, in particular, the student learns much from faculty members about values, attitudes, behaviors, and expectations of the discipline and the field (Austin and McDaniels, 2006; Weidman and Stein, 2003).

As alluded to earlier, however, these initial relationships with faculty members may be on a much more surface level than those the students will have with peers. As students begin to transform their visions of themselves in relation to authority and knowledge, their emphasis on "pleasing" the faculty member may diminish over time (Katz, 1976), but the inherent power differential between faculty member and student is still a persistent issue throughout the student's experience (Aguinis and others, 1996). Conversely, older students in particular may feel more of an initial connection to their faculty members than to their peers. One communications studies student explained, "I fit in better with the faculty than with some of the graduate students because they didn't know how to handle me, but the faculty did just because we're in the same age range."

Regardless of age, however, students desire an ever greater connection to faculty members early on. One history student shared, "I think there ought to be some greater interactions initially between students and faculty," and a math student commented, "It is really hard getting to know [professors]. Certainly seeing them outside the classroom experience makes a world of difference. If I see one professor out on the Frisbee field or if I see someone for coffee or something like that or if I'm eating lunch with a couple of the professors, that comfort level rises. It's nice to know there are such great professors there."

Structuring for faculty and student interactions in these early months is therefore greatly beneficial not only to students' sense of belonging in the department but also to their future socialization and success. Integration, in this sense, is vital to student persistence at the doctoral level (Lovitts, 2001; Tinto, 1993). Through informal social activities as well as more academically oriented brown bag seminars or talks, students can interact with faculty both inside and outside the academic environment. In addition, structuring for increased doctoral student interaction through shared office space for students with assistantships or student lounges may be helpful (Boyle and Boice, 1998). Taken together, forming healthy, professional relationships with faculty members is a key component of students' psychosocial development (Chickering and Reisser, 1993). Moreover, students' social identity may also develop through relationships with advisors who serve as mentors, particularly those from underrepresented populations such as women and students of color (Rentz, 2003; Zachary, 2000).

For part-time students, however, these relationships may be more difficult to build, and the absence of these relationships may have a detrimental effect on students' later success. Tinto (1993) asserted, "The difference between full-time and part-time attendance . . . is not merely a time commitment. It is also a difference in the degree to which one is able to become involved in the intellectual and social life of the student and faculty communities that undergird graduate education. Whereas the former may serve to extend time to degree completion, and only indirectly constrain persistence, the latter acts directly to undermine persistence by isolating the person from the intellectual and social life of the department" (p. 234).

Student Departure in Phase I

> It was really humiliating because I've always been the person that's like—in my family, we're all girls. I have two older sisters and we've all been raised to be very strong women and it was the first time I remember that I ever called up my parents and cried because I just couldn't deal. I wasn't sleeping, I had total anxiety all the time. I realized I had to go get help and for me going to talk to a total stranger and saying I had problems was like the worst thing ever, like I failed as a person, like I can't keep it together. You know?

> History student, leaving at the end of Phase I

Faced with an absence of support or being overwhelmed by the challenges present in Phase I, not all students make the successful transition to graduate school and depart from the degree program during this time. In fact, up to 40 percent of doctoral students who leave do so during this phase (Bowen and Rudenstine, 1992; Lott and Gardner, forthcoming). And although students leave for many reasons, we do know that some of the attrition that occurs during this time may be the result of a lack of coherent expectations on the part of the graduate program (Lovitts, 2001).

The literature on doctoral student attrition, however, discusses the difference between "good" and "bad" attrition; that is, attrition occurring earlier may be more beneficial for both the student and the program as neither party has yet fully invested or committed large amounts of resources or time to the experience (Bowen and Rudenstine, 1992; Golde, 1998). Although this observation may be true from the perspective of resources, the toll that this decision-making process may take on the student who chooses to depart can be immeasurable. Lovitts (2001) interviewed many students who left their doctoral programs and found both deep emotional and psychological stress as a result of this decision. She points out, "Leaving graduate schools is not just changing a job. It often involves changing a culture and redefining deeply held concepts and images of who one is and hoped to become" (p. 192). In this way, the identity development and psychosocial development of these individuals may be drastically challenged. Golde (1998) explains that many first-year students ask themselves four main questions relating to their mastery of the program and the changes necessary to succeed: (1) Can I do this? (2) Do I want to be a graduate student? (3) Do I want to do this work? (4) Do I belong here? Although some students may feel that leaving is absolutely the right choice for them and they feel their lives improved from making this decision (Lovitts, 2001), others, like the history student above, take this decision as a personal failure.

Conclusion

Taken together, the developmental challenges and opportunities that await doctoral students in this first phase can be both overwhelming and exhilarating. Psychosocially, doctoral students in Phase I must cope with the need to establish purpose and demonstrate their competencies to themselves, their faculty, and their peers. At the same time, the relationships students are forming with their peers and faculty members are inherently part of both their vocational goals and the need for establishing mature interpersonal relationships. Cognitively, Phase I requires that students begin to think more independently and make a commitment to these decisions. Moreover, the socialization and development that students experience in this phase are paramount to their success in the second and third phases of their development. Similarly, students' social identity development may be influenced by their coursework, particularly those students in disciplines where coursework and class-related discussions may challenge commonly held assumptions. Providing necessary support, clarity, and structure to assist students through these challenging times goes a long way in ensuring success not only in this phase but also in those to come. The following chapter discusses the development that occurs in Phase II, Integration.

Phase II: Integration

I don't feel like I'm a student anymore in the Ph.D. program. I feel like the faculty members make it seem like everybody is kind of equal. Everyone's experience is the same; everybody's experiences deserve the same respect and consideration.

Higher education student

My key to success has actually been my own drive, my own purpose.

English student

Pick your advisor based on how well you think you're going to get along with him because the relationship, you know, in doctoral education is extremely important.

Chemistry student

The stress of what was going to come at me was ridiculous . . . because you have no idea [what will be on your examination]. It scares you to death. I about went crazy. . . . I saw the doctor and I was put on antidepressants, as were probably half of the other students.

History student

AS STUDENTS TRANSITION FROM PHASE I TO PHASE II in their programs, they enter a period known as Integration. In this phase, students are in the midst of completing their coursework and preparing for the examinations that will allow them to become doctoral candidates. This chapter discusses the developmental challenges and sources of support present during this phase: establishing competency in subject matter through coursework, deepening peer relationships, establishing a relationship with an advisor, preparing for examinations, changing role from student to professional, departing the program as a result of a lack of support. The development that occurs as a result of and in relation to these challenges and opportunities is detailed below.

Challenge: Coursework

The classes were more challenging than in undergrad, obviously. I wasn't used to having to study as much and having to actually work for grades.

Psychology student

If I hadn't sought out the knowledge on my own, I wouldn't have gained anything from the course. I think you need to be a pretty self-directed learner, take it upon yourself to learn, be committed, commit yourself.

Higher education student

While students began their coursework in Phase I, students in Phase II are continuing to explore their cognitive, intellectual, and epistemological development through their coursework. In particular, as much as Phase I involves a transition from undergraduate to graduate expectations in relation to coursework but also in the student role, Phase II is a time when doctoral students begin to become truly immersed in the language and culture of the discipline. Furthermore, after transitioning through Phase I, students in Phase II are able to better understand the expectations needed to be successful in their coursework and in their disciplines.

With regard to cognitive and epistemological development, students in Phase II continue the explorations of the nature of knowledge and truth through their coursework and beginning forays into research. Take, for example, this quote from a Phase II student in higher education: "We were required to take a qualitative course and I'm fairly anal; I like being black and white. I don't do real well—well, I do better now with gray. How [the professor] explained it to me is that it's not the destination, it's the journey. That's something I've had to learn: it's not really an end point. I'm not going to stop learning, I'm going to continue to develop those skills hopefully until I retire. But it's the journey." His understandings of the nature of research and his changing views of the nature of knowledge (it is no longer black and white, rather gray) demonstrate his development with respect to both cognitive and epistemological development (Perry, 1968).

In addition, students are developing in relation to their competency and sense of purpose by successfully navigating their coursework (Chickering and Reisser, 1993). The difference between Phase I and Phase II students in this regard, however, is the transition they experience as they move from a view of success in doctoral experience as being able to master tangible skills such as writing and conducting research to one that encompasses more intangible understandings and habits of mind (Gardner, Hayes, and Neider, 2007). As shown in Exhibit 2, a few quotes from students in Phase I and Phase II illustrate these differences.

Although these four quotes represent only students from the field of higher education, they are the same types of conceptualizations heard over and over again from students in both Phases I and II, illustrating the higher complexity of thinking and, on a larger level, thinking about thinking itself.

Specifically, students begin seeing their roles differently in the classroom in Phase II. No longer are they just the student learning from the instructor; they begin to see themselves in a larger role of knowledge producer (Delamont, Atkinson, and Parry, 2000; Egan, 1989; Lovitts, 2001). For those students with academic aspirations, they may also begin to see the role they will play in dispensing this knowledge someday. One chemistry student related, "I'm studying to remember. I'm studying to *learn* the material. I'm studying to learn how to use it and apply it to what I'm doing." Similarly, a mathematics student explained the difference between undergraduate and doctoral students in their classes: "When they are finished with this class they might get a bachelor's degree. When you are finished with this class, it is toward something completely higher."

EXHIBIT 2
Phase I and II Student Cognitive Development

Phase I Student	Phase II Student
"Technology is definitely new for me. Another skill is definitely the basics of doing research. Definitely the research skills in terms of doing qualitative and quantitative research and understanding those processes. I think I further honed my writing skills."	"In graduate school we are taught to critically analyze the theories and articles, to question the assumptions and not take everything you read as fact or at face value. Asking what is the author trying to say? What are his or her assumptions? How would you analyze this? What would this mean in a different context? I mean, we would just literally pick things apart. It was fun to do that because you just had to think, you had to think these things through and think of different perspectives; to me that is very stimulating."
"Reading, writing, and research kind of to me are all the same thing."	"You don't just come into the program thinking that it is safe to say 'What if the author is not right?' Because you're not taught that in undergraduate; you're taught that whatever's written in the book must be tried and true. But what you find out as a Ph.D. student is that those are people's ideas and what they think and that a lot of times they put those ideas out there just so they can be deconstructed and made sense of and sort of toyed with. That's how people tend to be lifelong learners."

In addition, this transition to knowledge producer allows students to see themselves as more independent in their learning, realizing that they may need to seek out additional information and knowledge to be successful not only in the course but also in their upcoming dissertation research (Gardner, 2008c). Again, this self-directed view of learning is a central tenet of adult learning (Merriam and Clark, 2006).

Another result of the changing role the students begin to see is that of their larger role in society. One higher education student remarked, "It's like I know too much now. It's like I feel a responsibility because I know too much or I feel a sense of responsibility because if I want to know something I know how to find it. The fact that I know that I know, I feel a sense of responsibility." In this context, students are changing on another level of psychosocial development, particularly relating to developing integrity and purpose (Chickering and Reisser, 1993). The transition to this way of seeing themselves in response to the larger research dialogue in their field indicates a shifting transition in socialization and the early transition to Phase III.

Support: Peer Relationships

You need as many people around you as possible supporting you, just in terms of emotional support, like if you could live close to family and have friends.

English student

The people in my program were very supportive and we really networked together and really reached out for help because we were all going through a similar experience.

Psychology student

I can't praise my fellow graduate students enough.

Chemistry student

As much as development in coursework in Phase II is a continuation of what doctoral students gain from Phase I, the relationships the students have with their peers in Phase II are a continuation of the relationships they have begun to build in Phase I. Forming these relationships encompasses developmental competencies in psychosocial development, through the development of mature interpersonal relationships (Chickering and Reisser, 1993). Although these peer relationships are a continuation of peer relationships built in Phase I, these relationships become much more important to the students as they progress through Phase II, particularly in regard to their preparation for the next phase of their development: their advancement to candidacy.

What is truly remarkable is that many doctoral students actually speak more often and more positively about the support they receive from one another than from any other source (Gardner, 2007). The relationships students form with their peers during this phase are not only integral to their persistence but also often to their success in the third and final phase. So too will the relationships they build with their peers at this phase be vital to their coming success, as these individuals may become colleagues in their future profession.

A big part of the relationship development at this phase is built on the empathy that students receive from one another about their stresses, challenges, and concerns. One oceanography student explained, "I think other graduate students are usually very helpful because they've gone through a lot of it so I think talking to them they give you some really good advice." A history student shared, "Just knowing that someone's going through this with you at the same time and struggling with the same issues really helps keep you sane."

Despite the importance their peers play in their success, the literature about their role is relatively sparse. This lack of literature may be owing to the fact that the doctoral experience has traditionally been seen as a connection between student and advisor (Bargar and Mayo-Chamberlain, 1983; Berelson, 1960) or that of a solitary student independently creating knowledge through the dissertation experience (Baird, 1997).

Support: Advisor Relationship

My advisor has always been someone I couldn't imagine being without. She has always helped me through everything.

Communications student

If you don't get along with your advisor, your life can be hell.

Chemistry student

I've always heard that choosing an advisor is like choosing a marriage. You do have to get along with them at least, be able to communicate with [them] so that you can actually see eye to eye about your progress and your research and how things are going; otherwise, it's going to be a really miserable experience. Whether you like them or not, I don't know if that really matters, but I guess it wouldn't hurt.

History student

If the literature about the role of the graduate student peer relationship in doctoral education is sparse, the existing literature related to the importance of the advisor relationship is voluminous in comparison. Although some doctoral students choose their advisor on admission to their program or have a faculty member assigned to them on entrance to the program, many students make a conscious choice to work with one particular faculty member over another during this phase. Regardless of the length of time the student has been with his or her advisor, it is only during this phase that students truly develop a relationship with these faculty members.

First, a word on terminology. Depending on discipline and institution, many different terms are used for the role of the faculty member who guides the student through the doctoral experience and dissertation stage. Terms such as *chair, supervisor, director, advisor, major advisor,* and even *mentor* may all be used to describe the same role. Moreover, the terms *advisor* and *mentor* may be used interchangeably but may nevertheless represent quite distinct roles in the existing literature. For example, King (2003) differentiated by defining mentoring as a relationship that "suggests a level of personal interaction, nurture, and guidance that exceeds the requirements of 'good enough' research advising" (p. 15). "Rather than being concerned solely with the student's completing the dissertation or developing technical competence, the mentor is concerned with promoting a broader range of psychosocial, intellectual, and professional development" (p. 15). In this sense, this monograph distinguishes between advising and mentoring, with the more developed relationship between student and faculty member that of mentor.

The advising relationship between graduate student and faculty member has been shown to be of the utmost importance to graduate students' success and retention (Bargar and Mayo-Chamberlain, 1983; Barnes, forthcoming; Lovitts, 2001; Tinto, 1993; Zhao, Golde, and McCormick, 2005), and this relationship has been the focus of much critique and commentary throughout the history of graduate education in the United States. The role of the advisor in doctoral education includes myriad duties and dispositions, but some of the more cited include being accessible to students (Girves and Wemmerus, 1988; Hartnett, 1976; Lovitts, 2001), providing students with regular, positive feedback on their progress (Hartnett, 1976; Heiss, 1970; Sorenson and Kagan, 1967), showing care and concern for their students (Nettles and Millett, 2006; Zhao, Golde, and McCormick, 2005), being credible and trustworthy (Aguinis and others, 1996), treating students as colleagues or equals (Girves and Wemmerus, 1988; Heinrich, 1995), and being supportive (Abedi and Benkin, 1987; Zhao, Golde, and McCormick, 2005).

A relationship with an advisor, or chair, can begin as early as the first days in a program and therefore early in the socialization process. As previously stated, many graduate programs assign graduate students to faculty members, while other programs only accept students who have already been chosen to work with specific faculty members. Lovitts (2001) found in her study, however, that many graduate students who were assigned advisors on entering their program felt no connection with these faculty members. Nevertheless, the students tended to remain with these assigned advisors throughout their programs. When these students were asked why they had never changed advisors, they responded that it had never occurred to them as an option.

The relationship with the advisor has one of the greatest impacts on the graduate student and his or her future career (Baird, 1995; Clark and Corcoran, 1986; Girves and Wemmerus, 1988; Lovitts, 2001). The reputation of the potential advisor in the larger disciplinary field is likely to influence the future of the student, as a positive advisor relationship with an established scholar in the field, or the lack thereof, leads to accumulated advantage or disadvantage (Clark and Corcoran, 1986) over the career of the graduate student. In academe, in particular, the status and reputation of the advisor is often a contributing factor to the student's networking in the field, access to fellowships and scholarly opportunities, and future placement in professional positions (Clark and Corcoran, 1986).

Fischer and Zigmond (1998) identified several points graduate students should keep in mind when choosing an advisor: talk to other graduate students to discover their experiences with individual faculty members, and do not choose someone that the graduate student thinks he or she can merely survive but someone with whom the student can be a true partner. The graduate student should ask the faculty member several questions, including what he or she feels the student's role should be in generating research questions, his or her opinion about ownership of ideas and authorship on publications, and the advisor's definition of an adequate doctoral dissertation. The student should not shy away from asking the potential advisor about his or her policies on feedback, deadlines, and working styles, as these policies are all highly influential in the life of the graduate student in the time to come. Finally, Fischer and Zigmond stress that one person may not meet all the student's needs, and they encourage students to seek out a group of mentors from whom they can seek advice and guidance. Again, the relationship with the advisor is an important part of the graduate student's experience. Assisting students in the steps involved and questions to be asked when choosing an advisor is invaluable to students' future success in their programs and careers.

As these relationships are formed and developed throughout Phase II, students also develop mature interpersonal relationships as part of their psychosocial development (Chickering and Reisser, 1993). For underrepresented students, however, the mentoring relationship between student and advisor may have other effects on their development. For example, women who form advising relationships with male faculty members may gain just as many benefits from these relationships as their male peers (Hartnett, 1981; Schroeder and Mynatt, 1993), but issues concerning sexual harassment or power differentials may arise (Aguinis and others, 1996; Dziech and Weiner, 1990; Katz, 1976). Similarly, women students who seek out other women as advisors may receive increased benefits from these relationships related to those individuals having experienced similar challenges and development (Belenky, Clinchy, Goldberger, and Tarule, 1986; Gilligan, 1978; Josselson, 1973), but they may also face challenges related to competition (Heinrich, 1995) and accumulated disadvantage in the larger field (Clark and Corcoran, 1986).

Students of color, on the other hand, may seek out faculty of color for these mentoring roles (Tierney and Bensimon, 1996), assisting them in their own professional and identity development (Brown, Davis, and McClendon, 1999; Duncan, 1976; Ellis, 2001; Gay, 2004; Larke, Patitu, Webb-Johnson, and Young-Hawkins, 1999), but they may also find obstacles in underrepresented fields (Herzig, 2004a; MacLachlan, 2006).

Challenge: Examinations

The dissertation isn't going to be a barrier for me probably because I think the groundwork is already laid building on my thesis. For me it's more about getting through generals and making sure I'm fine there.

Higher education student

I think the purpose of the exam is to test our background knowledge in our own field. That's the purpose, I just don't know if it's the real one or not.

Electrical engineering student

The general exam was much more anxiety-provoking than any thesis or dissertation proposal or defense, and I think that's because it's just so subjective. There are no guidelines.

Psychology student

More than any other topic discussed with students, candidacy examinations are by far the most stressful and anxiety-producing issue for students in this phase. These examinations may be referred to as general examinations, preliminary examinations, qualifying examinations, or comprehensive examinations, depending on the discipline and the institution. Although other types of examinations may accompany the doctoral experience such as language examinations or qualifying examinations that occur during this phase, the examination that generally allows admission into candidacy is the focus of this section. The Council of Graduate Schools (2005) explains, "Admission to candidacy means that, in the judgment of the faculty, the doctoral student has adequate knowledge of the field and the specialty, knows how to use the academic resources, has potential to do original research autonomously, and presumably will complete the dissertation" (pp. 24–25). With this understanding in mind, it is perhaps not surprising that students feel much anxiety about this final hurdle before the dissertation.

What is interesting, however, is that although the Council of Graduate Schools is able to precisely define the purpose of the candidacy examination, very rarely are students able to do so. As evidenced in the quotes above, much of the stress that accompanies this part of Phase II is the result of the ambiguity and lack of clarity surrounding the examination. Indeed, Walker and others (2008) dedicate a significant portion of their text to discussing the candidacy examination's lack of clarity. From a developmental context, this examination is of paramount importance to the student. The examination not only represents a major rite of passage in which the student shifts from the identity of student to scholar but also is an important step in proving the student's merit and worth as a burgeoning scholar to faculty and peers. In this way, the examination exists as one of the final hurdles in the student's self-concept, sense of purpose, and feeling of competence (Chickering and Reisser, 1993).

Examinations are the stuff of lore for many students, however. The experience itself proves to be mythic in proportion, with even Phase I students wrought with fear about their ability to successfully pass through this doctoral rite of passage. One history student said, "Everyone I talked to and everyone I've known that's taken [the exam] says it's the worst thing in the world and you have all these doubts like you're not going to pass and it's really a hellish time." In actuality, students typically use words like "hellish" and "miserable" to describe the examination experiences (Gardner, 2007), with some students even discussing their need to seek counseling and take antidepressants to get through their examination stress. Moreover, many of the interviewed students who have considered leaving their programs or the students who were planning to leave thought about doing so in relation to their fear of success on this examination.

Challenge: Changing Role

I think my role is more connected to professors where they are more my mentors than they are just a professor. I think my role is to learn from them to see how they do things and then try and do like they do.

Higher education student

I saw myself moving from feeling like you're just a student, you're just in school, to thinking about it in terms of a career.

Communications student

Much like the first phase of the doctoral experience resulted in a transition in the student's role and expectations, Phase II encompasses several transitions in the student's role, including the shifting role from student to scholar produced through socialization. In particular, students experience several stages of socialization during Phase II, moving from what Weidman, Twale, and Stein (2001) refer to as the formal stage of socialization to the informal stage. They define the formal stage as one in which "students are inducted into the program, practice role rehearsal, and thereby determine their degree of fitness, observe and imitate expectations through role taking, and become familiar faces in the program" (p. 13) and the informal stage as one in which the student "learns of the informal role expectations" through "adept communication and immersion in the new culture. . . . [Although] some of this information comes from faculty, students tend to develop their own peer culture and social and emotional support system among classmates" (p. 14). We can see this shift in socialization roles moving from the formal student in coursework, learning the ropes of the new department and discipline in Phase I, to more intangible aspects of the role of student-scholar in Phase II. Likewise, we see the shifting relationships from Phase I to Phase II in relation to peers and faculty members, resulting in different understandings of the culture and its expectations.

During this phase, students may also see several changing aspects of their understanding of the academic culture. Specifically, they begin to see a different side of their faculty and begin to see a less idealized view of the academic world in general (Katz, 1976; Weidman, Twale, and Stein, 2001). A few quotes illustrate these transitions:

You don't know the politics of the department so I put together a committee where some people didn't like the other people and I didn't know. What

I continuously got caught up in was personality conflicts. You have to be a researcher and find out who doesn't like whom [English student].

It seems there is a lot of inter-department politics going on, which can be at the detriment of the students' learning and things like that. It's actually made me never want to be in academia [psychology student].

The faculty are often at each other's throats. . . . The divisions are obvious [history student].

I thought I would become an academic and definitely changed my mind quickly about that, and my experience here would definitely reinforce that I wouldn't want to be an academic. I don't see a lot of really happy faculty members to be honest [chemistry student].

Existing literature underscores the disillusionment that many students feel about the academic world, turning many off from the idea of pursuing positions in academe after graduation (Austin, 2002; Austin and McDaniels, 2006; Gaff, 2002; Nyquist and others, 1999).

At the same time, however, students may increase their professional socialization in quite positive ways through their involvement in assistantships as well as in local and national professional associations. Assistantships such as those in professional offices or in teaching or research provide students with professional socialization for future roles and provide them with opportunities to strengthen the skills and habits of mind they are developing during Phase II (Brown-Wright, Dubick, and Newman, 1997; Ethington and Pisani, 1993; Perna and Hodgins, 1996). Much like other parts of the graduate experience, students in assistantships gain relationships with others, strengthen their abilities and sense of purpose, and develop their abilities in relation to the role (Nyquist and Wulff, 1996).

With regard to professional involvement, Gardner and Barnes (2007) found that the involvement of graduate students is often developmental in and of itself, as students begin to take more active roles in professional associations during this phase. Through attending and presenting at conferences, students not only receive the opportunity to model some of the skills and traits necessary to be successful in the field but are also able to begin interacting with other scholars and professionals in their field outside their institution. This networking may also assist students in opening doors to future positions and career opportunities (Gardner and Barnes, 2007). This "trying on" of the professional role may be particularly helpful with regard to the student's burgeoning psychosocial development and the development of competence (Chickering and Reisser, 1993).

Student Departure in Phase II

I guess what continues to surprise me is how hard it is and why I can't figure out what [is] so hard. I think I've just determined that it's just emotionally taxing for some reason and part of it is that every time of day you're trying to defend yourself and I don't think it's very good for self-esteem, personally.

Chemistry student

I think that there's this bitterness that comes from being a graduate student in this department and maybe all departments. But I find here, in my experience, there's this bitterness that graduate school is self-defeating and soul-crushing. And when you turn to your fellow graduate school students and you say, 'I'm tired and I don't want to be here anymore and I don't know what to do, I'm frustrated,' nine out of ten times you get the reaction like, 'Yeah, I've been there. Want to get a drink?' You know? I guess there's camaraderie there, but it's not, I don't know, I couldn't say it's necessarily helpful.

History student

About 30 percent of students who begin doctoral programs leave during Phase II (Bowen and Rudenstine, 1992; Golde, 1998; Lott and Gardner, forthcoming). As many studies have pointed out, students rarely leave because of academic difficulties such as poor grades (Bowen and Rudenstine, 1992; Lovitts, 2001) but often because of myriad other reasons, including a lack of support to alleviate the many challenges prevalent in this phase.

Lovitts (2001) found that students who left during this phase may have left because of disappointment with the learning experience. Many hoped for more intellectual stimulation in their programs, and others may have been disappointed by the sense of a weeding-out process by the faculty in their early experiences. In Gardner's work (2008a), students who left during this phase may have done so because of a lack of connection with their advisor or inability to find or keep an advisor, their fear about being able to pass the examination, or failure of the examination after multiple attempts. Lovitts (2001) also found a number of students who left during this period because of financial reasons, with funding withdrawn, difficult to obtain, or insufficient.

The effect that departure at this phase may have on the student's development may be even more traumatic than for those students who leave in Phase I: Phase II students have by this point invested much more time, energy, and resources in the doctoral experience. Deep feelings of disappointment and emotional stress may therefore be prevalent for students who leave during this time (Lovitts, 2001).

Conclusion

As doctoral students culminate their experiences in Phase II through the examination experience, they begin to transform from the role of student to the role of candidate, thereby taking on a more professional scholarly role, one that is able to produce scholarship rather than simply the role of student. Psychosocially, students continue to form and manage relationships with peers and establish a deepening relationship with an advisor, an important part of their future success. Students must also continue to demonstrate competence in their coursework and successful completion of the examination to pass to Phase III, Candidacy. At the same time, students begin transitioning cognitively to the role of knowledge producer rather than knowledge consumer, requiring more sophisticated cognitive and epistemic abilities. Students may also undergo development in Phase II with regard to social identity, whether through continued challenges in their coursework or through deepening relationships with peers or an advisor. Upon successful completion of these challenges, students are able to advance to Phase III.

Phase III: Candidacy

When you transition from that dissertation stage where you don't have all the other students and your professor kind of hanging over you day-by-day, it's so profound, the change. You have to almost reinvent yourself.

English doctoral candidate

In some ways graduate school for me has been an educational experience, not just in the classroom, but just watching in the department because someday, believe it or not, I'm going to be faculty somewhere and I take all of these things, this sort of interpersonal sort of communication that happens, and try to internalize those and then I'll be able to take those with me later and, hopefully, will reflect on them.

History doctoral candidate

AFTER PASSING THE CANDIDACY EXAMINATION, the student becomes a doctoral candidate and progresses into the final phase of his or her program and development in the doctoral program. Phase III, also known as Candidacy, is the time during which the doctoral candidate begins to produce original research in the form of the dissertation. This chapter presents the final set of challenges and sources of support available to the doctoral student: transition to candidacy, the dissertation, the job search, transition to a professional role, and student departure.

Challenge: Transition to Candidacy

> Right now I feel like I'm an outsider. I know I'm a graduate student because I'm paying money to go to school but because I've completed coursework and I'm writing, I feel very disconnected from my colleagues and my peers.
>
> English doctoral candidate

Goodman, Schlossberg, and Anderson (2006) describe the many different kinds of transitions that adults may experience in relation to role changes. Specifically, they discuss differences between what they term "role gains" such as getting married, taking a job, or getting a promotion and "role losses" such as getting divorced or retiring (p. 62). Many doctoral students transitioning to candidacy may be experiencing both role gain and role loss.

For example, as students progress successfully through Phase II, they have built important and reliable relationships with peers and faculty. With regard to socialization, they have been exposed to and participated in the departmental and disciplinary cultures, allowing them to feel like a part of the community (Weidman, Twale, and Stein, 2001). When students advance to candidacy and transition into Phase III, however, this sense of community and the relationships they have formed may suddenly be removed. In fact, students in this phase of development may use words such as "lonely," "isolated," and "abandoned" to describe their status (Gardner, 2008c). A few quotes illustrate this point, like this one from a history student in Phase III who said, "There is this disconnect that you feel between sort of the department and you—it's obvious. There are little things you don't expect, like I didn't expect to lose contact with my advisor like I did," or another who mentioned, "When you get to the dissertation process, you're rarely around the department, you're not [a teaching assistant] any longer, so you don't have interaction with the program. . . . Now that I'm finishing the dissertation, I have basically very little interaction with anybody."

In many ways, however, this separation from the department becomes an important part of the transition to independent scholar. Students in most disciplines will be asked to complete an original piece of research, necessitating a reliance on themselves and their own skills and habits of mind (Council of Graduate Schools, 2005). Furthermore, this transition is vital to separating the scholar from the student, allowing the individual to seek a professional identity away from the institution and away from the role of student (Weidman, Twale, and Stein, 2001).

Therefore, in and of itself, this transition is the transition to independence. This topic has just begun to be explored in the larger body of literature (Gardner, 2008c; Lovitts, 2005, 2008), but the transition to independence can also be a difficult one for the student to make in relation to the loss of relationships as well as the need for self-direction, self-monitoring, and self-motivation. No one may be available to guide the student and tell him or her what needs to be done and when it is due or to provide continuous feedback on his or her progress. Inherent in this transition then is also cognitive development (Katz, 1976), as the student begins to separate from the authority figure of the advisor to the authority invested in self.

Challenge: The Dissertation Experience

I don't know what I'm doing. There's no class on how to write a dissertation. The dissertation is so different from what you're accustomed to and the most intimidating factor, and what has stilted my writing so much is that I don't know what I'm doing.

English student

The dissertation to me was the final check of being able to combine heart and head to know what you feel, what you believe to be true, and to infuse that and to say it with your voice. This whole process of going through the courses, the seminars, the GA experience—all that has been about finding my voice. Maybe that's what orientation should say. We should say to graduate students coming in, 'This whole process is really about you finding your voice and once you find your voice, you will have mastered what it takes to succeed in this program.'

Higher Education doctoral candidate

The doctoral dissertation is the "final product of years of study and independent research. Successful completion of the dissertation and award of the Ph.D. [certify] that the degree recipient has the capabilities and training necessary for independent scholarly work" (Lovitts, 2007, p. 3). Much like the trepidation and mythology that surround the candidacy examination in Phase II, anxiety is very much part of the long-awaited dissertation experience for many doctoral students. Upon reaching candidacy, students are often referred to as ABD, or all but dissertation. This title, however, is deceiving. The doctoral candidate may very well have finished everything but the dissertation, but the dissertation itself is by no means a simple exercise. As one chemistry student related, "If it were easy, everyone would have a Ph.D."

With regard to anticipatory socialization (Weidman, Twale, and Stein, 2001), students are well aware of the concept they understand to be the dissertation, but, similar to the graduate student experience itself, much ambiguity and confusion exist about the actual process and what is entailed in completing this exercise (Katz, 1997; Lovitts, 2001). The idea of writing what is in effect a book is not only intimidating to doctoral students but also anxiety producing (Heiss, 1970). For the majority of doctoral students, it will be the biggest academic project, both in length and depth, they have ever undertaken in their lives. The effects of the pressure to produce such a product, particularly on top of the recent transition they have begun to make to independence, may be downright paralyzing for many students. One need only to see the litany of self-help books and Web sites (see, for example, Bolker, 1998; Bryant, 2003) offering advice to doctoral students about writing and completing the dissertation to see that it is no easy task and may cause many students to feel stymied.

Before the writing can even begin, however, the student must choose a research topic and question. This process alone is often one of the most difficult for students (Bowen and Rudenstine, 1992; Gardner, 2008c; Katz, 1997; Lovitts, 2001; Nerad and Miller, 1997) and requires a great deal of understanding not only about the discipline but also about required research methodologies and study construction. This process is also one that the student undertakes collaboratively with his or her advisor and, in many cases, the dissertation committee. Depending on the discipline, the topic may have been chosen early in the program as a part of the candidacy examination or not until the student reaches candidacy (Council of Graduate Schools, 2005; Lovitts, 2007). Regardless, the dissertation stands as the ultimate test of the student's knowledge gained throughout all earlier doctoral program experiences (Council of Graduate Schools, 2005) and represents the ultimate psychosocial development with regard to the development of competence in the field (Chickering and Reisser, 1993) and the motivational skills needed to persist through completion (Green, 1997).

What follows in most disciplines is generally the dissertation proposal. Although it may be a formal or informal process, a lengthy document or an abbreviated one, this step of the dissertation process allows the student's committee to offer advice on the upcoming study (Lovitts, 2007). "Approval of the proposal—the topic, method, and scope—serves as a kind of contract, which, if fulfilled, almost always guarantees that the student will be awarded the Ph.D." (p. 67). This period of the dissertation process can take weeks to months, depending on the discipline and its requirements for fulfillment.

Upon approval of the proposal, the student then begins the actual study, including collecting data, analyzing data, and then writing the final document. Again, depending on the discipline, this part of the process may take many months to many years. The dissertation is the key point during which the student transforms from being a knowledge consumer to a knowledge producer (Katz and Hartnett, 1976). The writing process can be a debilitating experience for students who are not prepared for it (Lovitts, 2001). Earlier development of skills and competency in writing and research are helpful with regard to psychosocial development (Chickering and Reisser, 1993), but the stamina required to persist throughout multiple drafts of the product also indicates the student's clarified purpose (Chickering and Reisser, 1993) in reaching this goal. Students may also feel effects on their ego development (Weathersby, 1981) as faculty members critique their writing efforts (Weidman, Twale, and Stein, 2001).

Upon completion of the task, students are generally asked to defend their final product to their committee, who have typically had time to review the completed dissertation before meeting. At the successful completion of this experience, students are conferred the title of "doctor." Interestingly, many students remark about the anticlimactic nature of this experience (Gardner, 2005), expecting to feel something more than the let down they typically feel after this event.

It should be noted, however, that the requirements to pass from candidacy to completion are not lockstep. Indeed, many students struggle with the ambiguity that the dissertation experience entails. Often, questions abound regarding how long it will take, how long the document should be, and what it should look like (Lovitts, 2007), and rarely are students given definitive answers. As previously stated, the dissertation experience in some fields may last anywhere from months to decades (Lovitts, 2007), and the support students receive throughout the process is vital to their success.

Challenge: Isolation

One of the biggest challenges facing students who begin the dissertation is the isolation they feel. Leaving the camaraderie of peers in coursework and through the possible transition away from an assistantship position may result in yet another troubling aspect of the dissertation experience. Many students feel unprepared for their sudden isolation, and without regular meetings with an advisor to assuage this isolation, many students may feel what they have described as "orphaned" or "abandoned." Students have also described feelings of "being lost" or "floating around" as they spend months trying to find structure and direction amid this sudden transition to independence (Gardner, 2008c). In one way, we might see the transition students experience during the final phase of their development as a huge identity shift, resulting in the need for what may be considered a grieving process. Indeed, Goodman, Schlossberg, and Anderson (2006) talk about the need for support to successfully navigate the difficult transitions in adulthood but also mention that during times of transition, great disruptions of support systems may abound.

Support: The Dissertation Advisor

During the dissertation experience, therefore, the supportive role of the faculty mentor or dissertation advisor becomes paramount. In many ways, the relationship between the student-candidate and the advisor undergoes a major transition. Whereas the student may rely greatly on the advisor for advice and guidance during Phase II and throughout the beginning of Phase III, he or she begins to transition to the role of colleague by the end of the dissertation experience as student transforms into scholar, effectively becoming a member of the profession at the culmination of the doctoral program. This shift in psychosocial identity (Chickering and Reisser, 1993) results also in a shift of the socialization process (Weidman, Twale, and Stein, 2001) and a shift in ego development (Weathersby, 1981) as the student's view of the advisor changes from authority figure to colleague.

In the existing literature, the doctoral advisor plays an integral role in the successful completion of the dissertation. Katz (1997) describes the advisor's contributions during the dissertation process as assisting the student to find a manageable topic, setting a reasonable time line, and assisting the student to complete the dissertation in a reasonable amount of time. Tinto (1993) also points out that although previous phases may have included relationships with more faculty members, the dissertation experience results in a more directed relationship between one faculty member, or the advisor, and the student. "Consequently, persistence at this stage may be highly idiosyncratic in that it may hinge largely if not entirely upon the behavior of a specific faculty member" (p. 237).

In addition, as a result of the increased importance of the advisor's role at this stage, issues of social identity may also play a part in the student's success. For example, differences in race and gender may impede a successful relationship between the student and advisor (Duncan, 1976; Schroeder and Mynatt, 1993) and therefore lead to difficulties in successful completion of the dissertation. Moreover, the development of social identity students may experience as a result of their earlier doctoral experiences or issues that arise in their relationships with faculty members in this phase may also serve to further complicate an already challenging time (Gardner, 2008b).

Challenge: The Job Search

The lack of opportunities is a major obstacle. . . . I'm kind of stymied and I didn't realize that was really part of the game in history departments.

I didn't realize that would have happened or I would have picked a different field.

History doctoral candidate

I think once you get it, it goes back to that socialization process for prospective faculty members. I mean, there [are] certain things you need to do to be successful. If you want to be successful, you'll start pursuing some of those opportunities, inquiring about them. So after I realized the type of institution I wanted to work at, what I want to do as far as a research agenda, I started thinking more about the end result and how I could get there. So I think the farther along in the program, the more I engage with this.

Higher education student

Many full-time students also begin the job search in Phase III. For many, juggling the completion of the dissertation while "being on the market" can be doubly stressful. Finding a postdoctoral position in academia, in research fields, or the government may require many months of hard work, time, and dedication. Students often rely greatly on their advisor in this process for assistance as an advocate and often a reference, again furthering the professional socialization that occurs (Weidman, Twale, and Stein, 2001).

Another aspect of this challenging part of Phase III is the balance that students may need to seek when searching for a job while also trying to complete their dissertation. For students with familial responsibilities or full-time positions, this need for balance may be even more acute. This balancing of duties and responsibilities is yet another part of the student's ego development (Weathersby, 1981) and psychosocial development (Chickering and Reisser, 1993).

Added to the stress of this process is the often difficult job market for those seeking academic positions (Jones, 2003; LaPidus, 1997). Although some fields may have an overabundance of positions, others, like those in the humanities, often experience a glut of graduates for few positions (Kuh, 1996). As the history student's comment above illustrates, the added stress of finding a position in academia can be overwhelming. Taken together, the skills developed and the understandings gleaned from the student's socialization process throughout the graduate program will assist him or her in finding and keeping a professional position after graduation (Tinto, 1993; Weidman, Twale, and Stein, 2001).

Challenge: Transition to Professional Role

I think my role as an undergraduate student was really as a receiver—on the catching end of information—and there was the pitcher who was my professor and my job was to adequately and effectively catch the information being handed to me and pretty much throw it back in the same format it was given to me in, not to alter it, not to shape it, not to try to add or take away anything from it, but to give back the exact same ball that was pitched to me. And that was what I was graded on and evaluated on. As a Ph.D. student, if I had pitched back the exact same ball that had been handed to me, then that would have been grounds for failure. As a graduate student, the emphasis for me was to take the ball that was pitched to me, analyze not just the ball but the methods—why it was pitched to me, why am I in the position to receive the ball in the first place, and why is the professor even in [his] position to pitch the ball, who else is catching, who else is on my team. I mean, it was a much broader concept. I got to look at the whole game of baseball as opposed to standing there and catching a ball and pitching it back and never questioning that process, but just doing it. So I got to question the process. I got to play with that a little bit, which to me was much more engaging, much more active. I was much more actively involved in my learning. And also just taking that ball and adding to it, shaping it differently, taking away from it what I needed, and if I decided in the end to return it, then having a sound reason and being able to defend why I returned that ball in the condition that I returned it. To me, that's the difference for me as a learner: I had to make the decision. It wasn't just said to me, 'Okay, I'm pitching you a ball, now return it to me.' It was, 'I'm pitching you a ball, now what are you going to do with it?'

Graduating doctoral candidate in education

This student's comment illustrates the full scope of the development the doctoral student undergoes from the beginning of the program until the end. It encompasses cognitive, psychosocial, social identity, adult, epistemological, and professional development. Her baseball metaphor also presents the transitions she has experienced from undergraduate to graduate education. She now situates herself as undergoing one final transition as she is leaving: she is now no longer the student but now she is a professional, joining the ranks of the other doctorates before her and contributing to the larger research conversation.

In the final part of the development in Phase III, students transition once again. In this final transition, individuals leave the student role and become a colleague. They transition to what Weidman, Twale, and Stein (2001) term the personal stage of the graduate student socialization process in which "students form a professional identity. . . . They separate themselves from the department in search of their own identity. Through this process . . . students are to realize that their program is only preparatory to their professional goal, not the real thing" (pp. 14–15).

Students who have been enrolled part time throughout the duration of their program may not experience this transition in the same way that those who have been full time throughout their programs may experience it. Socialization for part-time students may not entail a transition in role in both the academic and the professional setting. As previously stated, the literature examining the socialization of part-time doctoral students is sparse, if not altogether absent; certainly, however, the relief from completing a multiyear program (which for part-time students in education, for example, may entail ten years or longer [Katz, 1997]) is tangible for these individuals.

Regardless of enrollment status, upon completion of the program these individuals assume the role of what the Carnegie Initiative on the Doctorate refers to as a "steward of the discipline" (Walker and others, 2008). They describe this sense of stewardship "as encompassing a set of knowledge and skills, as well as a set of principles. The former ensures expertise and the latter provides the moral compass. A fully formed scholar should be capable of *generating* and critically evaluating new knowledge; of *conserving* the most important ideas and findings that are a legacy of past and current work; and of understanding how knowledge is *transforming* the world in which we live, and engaging in the transformational work of communicating their knowledge responsibly to others" (p. 12). This definition presupposes the same types of developmental attributes that were discussed in this monograph and that we can see in the student's quote above. Becoming a steward of the discipline, in this sense, is not relegated to one type of professional setting (for example, academia or government) or to one kind of student (part time or full time) but rather represents the larger discipline and field of research particular to the culture from which the student has graduated. Thus, we see the steward of the discipline realizing the totality of the development one could attain in the doctoral program.

Student Departure in Phase III

Nobody tells you how to do this. Nobody teaches you how to do research. You come in and you're expected to know how to figure out what the next step is. You're expected to know if someone presents you with a problem, how you're going to go about solving it. For me, I didn't know how to do that.

Chemistry doctoral candidate

Given the large amount of pressure and dedication inherent in the dissertation experience, the job search, and the transition to the professional role, it is perhaps not surprising that so many students do not complete Phase III. In fact, about 30 percent of all students who will leave their programs do so during this time. The devastating effect that student departure in this phase of the doctoral experience can have both on the student and the program is immeasurable, particularly considering the amount of time, energy, resources, and effort that have been dedicated to the process (Lovitts, 2001).

The amount of time it takes to complete a dissertation varies considerably, ranging from only one year in some disciplines to many years, particularly in the humanities (Bowen and Rudenstine, 1992). During this time, students are under inordinate internal and external pressure to complete the degree. In English, where the dissertation is often a multiyear experience, one student said, "There's another level of pressure coming from all the people who say,

'When will you graduate?' As if, you know, this whole dissertation process is kind of like a four-year degree where you take a set number of hours and you're done; it just doesn't work that way. I think that puts another level of pressure on you because it can make you feel inadequate when every semester you're pushing it back another semester."

In her study, Lovitts (2001) interviewed only one student who had begun his dissertation before leaving the program. His reason for leaving was that he took a full-time job that distracted him from the process. The duration of the dissertation experience as well as the lack of funding that accompanies a lengthy experience, particularly in the humanities (Bowen and Rudenstine, 1992), may create a no-win situation for many students.

Lack of adequate and dependable advising may also contribute to students' decisions to depart at this phase (Bowen and Rudenstine, 1992). As the advising relationship in this phase of development is one of the main sources of support the student has (Katz, 1997), dissertation advisors and committee members should be cognizant of the effects their attention, or lack thereof, may play in students' success.

Conclusion

Taken together, the development occurring throughout Phase III encompasses the time spent in candidacy at the doctoral level or the culmination of the student's graduate program. The skills and habits of mind accumulated throughout their program as well as the development experienced allows doctoral students in this phase to leave behind the role of student and take on the new role of steward of the discipline. In this way, through gaining independence and transitioning to the role of steward, the student is no longer student but a representative of the discipline to the larger world. From a developmental perspective, the sources of challenge and support in the student's life require that he or she attain psychosocial development with regard to maintaining purpose and developing competence in his or her field, while cognitively, he or she must become the producer of original knowledge, requiring the most advanced epistemological and cognitive development. As doctoral students manage the changing peer and advisor relationships, they are also transitioning through important adult development. Deepening relationships with advisors as well as the challenges introduced by a job search may also influence social identity development of the doctoral student in Phase III.

The final chapter discusses the totality of the doctoral student development model presented in the monograph and leaves readers with an overview of the possible implications of this model for policy, practice, and further research.

Summary and Recommendations

I think it's a wonderful thing to have a Ph.D. and I think that it's a good experience. It certainly teaches you a lot about yourself and other people in your life, but it's also very hard.

Graduating chemistry student

It's about you. It should ultimately be about you and your learning. And to make sure that that's happening, whether that means you're going to other professors to get help or other colleagues to get help, you know, whatever it is that you need, that you make sure that it happens because nobody here is going to make it happen for you. It's about you—that's why you came to graduate school.

Graduating history student

Now moving on to a different phase of my educational career (because it is still my education), I have a different place in that continuum. I'll still be a part of a community of scholars regardless of where I go, even though now the role that I play will not be so much as a student as it will be a faculty member; but I'll still be a learner.

Graduating higher education student

THE FINAL CHAPTER IN THIS MONOGRAPH provides an overview of the model of doctoral student development and proposes recommendations for policy and practice in doctoral education. Much like the organization of the monograph, this final chapter is presented in the context of the phases of doctoral student development and includes suggestions for policy and practice in each phase. It concludes with a broad discussion of the research that remains to be addressed in relation to doctoral student development.

Implications for Phase I

Phase I includes the time of admission and the first experiences in the doctoral program. Students in Phase I experience many transitions, whether through new expectations, new relationships, or even a new environment or location. The following tasks and issues arise with respect to doctoral student development in this phase:

Students focus on making the transition to doctoral studies and to doctoral student expectations.

Students are concerned with forming relationships with peers and faculty members that will later assist them in their career development and socialization.

Coursework begins, and students are often faced with different epistemological and intellectual challenges as they begin to transition from being knowledge consumers to knowledge producers.

Full-time students may also begin assistantships in Phase I, which will greatly enhance the development of skills and knowledge needed for a future career.

Part-time students may have to deal with issues related to balance between career and external commitments.

Personal identity development as it relates to sociocultural demographics may also be influenced by factors both internal to and external to the graduate program.

Making the Transition and Forming Relationships

An important part of the initial transition to doctoral education should include a comprehensive orientation. Orientation programs can provide answers to early questions as well as facilitate the forming of relationships among peers and with faculty members in the program. Administrators and faculty members should keep in mind, however, that they should not inundate already overwhelmed students with endless details and paperwork; rather, comprehensive Web sites and handbooks, which can be introduced to students at orientation, can provide information during later phases that may not be as vital as the information they require to successfully navigate the first days and months of the program. The paperwork and resources that exist, however, should be clear, and administrators should ensure that they are up to date. Allowing advanced students to regularly review these documents may assist in this regard.

Orientation or induction programs should also include informal components that allow students to meet one another and to interact with the faculty members who will teach their courses and may serve as dissertation chairs or committee members. Informal get-togethers allow for the social integration that is necessary for early success in the socialization process (Weidman, Twale, and Stein, 2001), thus leading to retention (Tinto, 1993). Not all students, however, are full-time students. With this fact in mind, structuring gatherings and events during evenings and weekends and allowing for partners and children to be present at these gatherings may assist part-time students to feel more welcome while normalizing their lives outside the classroom.

Another means of encouraging student interaction is through the establishment of a peer mentoring program, wherein a more advanced student in the program can be paired with a new student, allowing for informal advising and connection. Students rely greatly on these peer relationships, particularly early during their programs (Gardner, 2007). In the same way, students with assistantships can be placed together in office spaces that encourage interaction among multigenerational doctoral students, again allowing for informal mentoring and social integration (Walker and others, 2008).

An additional part of Phase I is the transition students experience regarding the expectations of doctoral-level education. Making clear both explicit expectations (such as reading load or level of writing ability) and the implicit expectations (the need for increased independence and the necessity for students to join professional associations) during orientation and throughout coursework goes a long way toward clarifying a great deal of the ambiguity that surrounds doctoral education (Katz, 1976). Similarly, clarifying the steps and progression of doctoral education as well as providing details and clarification on particularly stressful components such as the examination may alleviate many concerns and much trepidation. These expectations and guidelines can be made clear, however, only when they are clear to the faculty and the department. Facilitating discussions to clarify these details and expectations may be challenging but will certainly assist not only students but also faculty in the long run (Walker and others, 2008).

Nerad and Miller (1996) also suggest first-year evaluations of students in which faculty gather to discuss the student's progress and then meet with the student to determine the progress in the vital first year as well as in subsequent years. Regular feedback of this type allows students to explicitly understand their progress and to facilitate their understanding of the shifting expectations in doctoral education.

Coursework

Through their coursework, students may also undergo transitions in how they view knowledge and their role in the educational experience. Courses and experiences that encourage students to delve more deeply into epistemological theory and understandings may facilitate such development (Baxter Magolda, 1996; Elkana, 2006; Pallas, 2001). Similarly, Walker and others (2008) encourage the use of journal clubs and informal discussion groups to heighten students' interactions on discipline-specific issues and allow for the cross-generational student interaction that is a key part of this phase of development. In addition, creating opportunities to foster what the Carnegie Initiative on the Doctorate has referred to as "collaborative learning" (Walker and others, 2008), in particular, serves students and faculty alike in developing learning-rich communities of practice.

Assistantships

Many full-time students may also begin assistantships during this first phase. Although these assistantships may involve teaching, research, or general university services, development in how the student sees herself or himself in relation to this position and the skills needed in this setting is paramount to the student's future socialization and success (Brown-Wright, Dubick, and Newman, 1997; Ethington and Pisani, 1993; Holberg and Taylor, 1996; Korinek, Howard, and Bridges, 1999; Nyquist and Wulff, 1996). Again, providing comprehensive orientation sessions before the beginning of the assistantship and regular feedback on the student's performance is pivotal to their success (Nyquist and Wulff, 1996). Peer interaction such as occurs through shared office space, allowing for informal mentoring and guidance, can also be a helpful part of the student's development (Boyle and Boice, 1998).

Balancing Life Responsibilities

All students also experience transitions relative to balancing life responsibilities, but this transition may be even more acute for part-time students (Davis and McCuen, 1995). These individuals need to balance work and school as well as relationships inside and outside the academic environment. Again, providing mentoring programs that pair more advanced students who have experienced this transition with incoming students may ease this transition. Moreover, support groups and student organizations may also be helpful in identifying others who have experienced this transition and learning from their experiences. In a similar vein, workshops on time management and counseling services on campus may be helpful for all students in this phase.

Considering Self

As part of the transition experienced in Phase I, students also undergo personal identity development with regard to psychosocial tasks and challenges (Chickering and Reisser, 1993), but for underrepresented students, this development may take on a different aspect altogether. Students who may be entering departments where they are underrepresented among the student and faculty population may have difficulties establishing relationships with those who share similar sociocultural characteristics (Ellis, 2001; Margolis and Romero, 1998; Soto Antony and Taylor, 2004). When added to the levels of challenge apparent in Phase I already, these issues can be overwhelming. Again, mentoring programs within the program and throughout the university and graduate student organizations and other activities that facilitate interaction among underrepresented populations may assist students in finding others with shared experiences and backgrounds (Brown, Davis, and McClendon, 1999; Grant-Vallone and Ensher, 2000; Larke, Patitu, Webb-Johnson, and Young-Hawkins, 1999). In addition, occasions that provide networking opportunities with faculty members and other mentors on the campus and beyond can be helpful. Similarly, policies that consider hiring more underrepresented faculty and staff members as well as those who consider these sociocultural factors in admitting students may be helpful with regard to retention and success in the academic environment (Trower and Chait, 2002; Turner, 2002).

Implications for Phase II

Phase II encompasses the period known as Integration, the time spent mainly in coursework before advancing to candidacy but also the time during which students experience the following developmental tasks and challenges:

Coursework challenges students' competence and promotes identity development as a burgeoning scholar.

Students strengthen bonds with peers through coursework and out-of-class experiences.

Students begin to form more connections with faculty members, often choosing an advisor during this phase.

The candidacy examination remains a final hurdle before the dissertation and is often the most stressful period of time for the students in their programs.

The students' role in the department and in the discipline also begins to transition to the role of both student and burgeoning professional, a time during which more professional socialization occurs.

Coursework

Students continue to develop competency and purpose through their coursework, an inherent part of psychosocial development (Chickering and Reisser, 1993). During this time, the epistemological and cognitive development that began in Phase I may now begin to influence the students' understanding of themselves in relation to becoming knowledge producers rather than solely knowledge consumers. This type of development can be facilitated through increased opportunities to conduct research with faculty and through research opportunities in coursework early in the doctoral experience (Walker and others, 2008). In addition, collaborative learning opportunities with peers and with faculty such as through research projects and assistantships may also stimulate development.

Peer Relationships

The relationships the students begin to form in Phase I continue and are deepened in Phase II. Much like students may benefit from peer mentoring from more advanced peers in Phase I, students in Phase II may benefit from peer relationships with those students in Phase III at this time. Particularly in relation to preparation for the examination experience, students' fears and concerns about this event and about the transition to Phase III may be assuaged by such relationships. Moreover, students in Phase II may also begin serving as mentors for Phase I students, again allowing for more socialization (Weidman, Twale, and Stein, 2001) and social integration (Tinto, 1993).

Advisor Relationship

During Phase II, many students may choose an advisor with whom they will work on both the examination and their dissertation research. This relationship is a vitally important one that both the student and faculty member should weigh carefully (Bargar and Mayo-Chamberlain, 1983; Fischer and Zigmond, 1998). Therefore, allowing for student-faculty interaction before this decision may go a long way in facilitating better connections and fostering relationships between these individuals. In the sciences, it may be done through structured lab rotations, allowing students to spend a month or so in different faculty members' labs before choosing an advisor (Gardner, 2007), or through seminars that introduce students to faculty members' research and advising style. Again, informal opportunities for interaction are also important to students' understandings of faculty members, their personalities, and their advising styles. Students also rely strongly on each another for advice in this regard (Gardner,

2007), so previous suggestions for student interaction may also be beneficial. Several popular texts also include checklists and helpful hints for students to use when considering an advisor (Peters, 1997; Rossman, 2002), which may be of some use to students early in their programs. Therefore, although Web sites and handbooks that describe faculty members' work and background may supplement these efforts, they cannot replace the human element in forming these relationships among students and faculty members.

Once the relationship has been formed, regular meetings to provide feedback and connection throughout both Phases II and III are important in developing this relationship and building a strong foundation for the intense experience of Phase III.

The Examination

To prepare for the stress and anxiety produced by the candidacy examination, departments and programs can provide several sources of support and structure for their students. First, clear expectations and purposes of the examination should be transmitted to students early in their programs. With this clarity, students can better prepare and can better meet the expectations of faculty. Again, to communicate the expectations to students, the faculty must first agree on them, so structuring these conversations in the program or department may be a useful venture (Walker and others, 2008). Second, access to test banks or previous examination questions may be helpful for students to understand the types of questions that may be asked of them. Third, assisting students in forming study groups not only assists them in preparing for the exam but also in strengthening important peer relationships. Finally, programs may wish to consider alternate formats for the examinations that allow for success among different learning styles (Baxter Magolda, 1989). Again, facilitating discussions among faculty and students about the purpose and structure of this often difficult experience may be greatly helpful in myriad ways.

Changing Role

The overarching development occurring in Phase II also lends itself to the changing role of the student in the program and the discipline. The socialization occurring at this phase begins to transform the individual from the role of student to the role of professional. Students become much more integrated into the departmental environment and the larger discipline at this time and may become more aware of the political dimensions of the profession. This political aspect of the academic culture may contribute to feelings of disillusionment about the environment as well (Austin, 2002; Nyquist and others, 1999). Although students should not be shielded from this integrative period of the socialization process, faculty should be cautioned from overinvolving students in their conflicts and personal issues. As the students' quotes earlier illustrate, these conflicts create tension among students and complicate their often already challenging experiences. Students can still become socialized to disciplinary and departmental functions through participation in departmental governance and decision making (Walker and others, 2008) as well as through participation in assistantship positions (Nyquist and Wulff, 1996) and professional organizations and associations (Gardner and Barnes, 2007).

Implications for Phase III

Phase III encompasses the time generally referred to as "candidacy." This period includes the following developmental challenges and issues:

Transition to candidacy, taking on the role of independent researcher;

The dissertation experience, including the time from proposal through culmination of the research;

The job search, particularly for full-time students; and

The final transition to the role of professional and the separation from the department and role of the student.

Transition to Candidacy
As discussed in "Phase II: Integration," the transition to candidacy is the first of several challenging issues in this final phase of doctoral student development. The student begins working on his or her dissertation and therefore begins shifting from student to candidate and then from student to scholar (Council of Graduate Schools, 2005). This time can also be a lonely one for many students who will complete the majority of the dissertation work in solitude

(Katz, 1997). In this way, the transition to candidacy can be difficult for students as they learn to self-direct and self-structure for success as well as transition away from their dependence on peers. Therefore, providing opportunities for informal interaction among peers for students in this phase can be helpful as well as other types of dissertation writing support groups (Walker and others, 2008).

The Dissertation Experience

Related to the changing role from student to candidate, students also must shift to their work on the dissertation. Because of the independent nature of the task, students may feel lost, surrounded in ambiguity, and directionless (Gardner, 2008c). Similarly, the shift away from dependence on peer relationship to an increasing dependence on the advisor relationship may require some adjustment. Providing opportunities for student interaction and regular feedback and check-ins during this phase helps students through much of the ambiguous nature of this time. In addition, some students may even choose to audit classes or to remain working in assistantships to allow them some connection to the community. And although doctoral candidates may not need these support structures throughout the entire third phase, these structures may be helpful during the initial transition period. Regularly scheduled meetings to check in with the student may be not only necessary but also helpful to students and their advisors, providing necessary and timely feedback but also some structure in this ambiguity-laden time (Katz, 1997). Some campuses have also developed intensive multiday workshops or "boot camps" to assist students in finding structure and motivation to complete the dissertation (Nerad and Miller, 1997) as well as the dissertation support groups mentioned earlier. Finally, Lovitts (2007) has developed several useful guides for restructuring the dissertation experience by discipline, providing more explicit guidelines that detail the requirements, expectations, and rubrics for different aspects of the dissertation. Purposeful conversations among graduate faculty around these explicit guidelines may assist not only students but also faculty.

The Job Search

Although the support for a successful job search should begin much earlier than Phase III, it is nevertheless the time that the majority of students who will seek full-time employment after graduation begin their search. Again, providing early opportunities in Phase I and Phase II for students to explore the multiple career paths available to them and to prepare themselves with the required experiences for these positions is helpful in this regard. Workshops on topics such as skill building (University of Chicago, 2002), developing an effective curriculum vitae, interviewing, and negotiating job offers (Golde, 1999) may be very helpful during Phases II and III. Similarly, students may need assistance in balancing their completion of the dissertation with the job search, perhaps through time management workshops or through regularly scheduled check-ins with the advisor.

Transition to Professional Role

Finally, students begin to transition away from the role of student and candidate to the role of professional. The final stages of graduate school socialization end, and those who will begin a new position soon start a transition to the socialization of this new position and new culture. Exit interviews with graduating students may be helpful in learning more about their needs and concerns to assist in better structuring success for future students. In addition, providing celebratory events that are open to the entire department provides Phase I and Phase II students with anticipatory socialization for their future success and allows for the symbolic culmination of this transition from student to professional.

Implications for Future Research

Although more scholarship is conducted on doctoral students today than ever, it is evident that this population is still understudied. In many ways, this monograph may serve to create more questions than answers. Given the burgeoning area of scholarship in the area of doctoral education and the sparsely studied area of doctoral student development, the following section proposes general areas of scholarship and inquiry. Posited as research questions, the following section presents the implications for future research on the seven main areas of developmental literature: (1) psychosocial development, (2) adult development, (3) social identity development, (4) cognitive-structural development, (5) professional development, (6) campus-environment dynamics, and (7) student departure and success (McEwen, 2005). An important overriding consideration is that future scholarship should be conducted on all populations, including the different populations discussed earlier such as international students, part-time students, students with varied sociocultural backgrounds, and students in different disciplinary and institutional cultures.

Psychosocial Development

What specific aspects of psychosocial development are affected by the different doctoral experiences? Could added dimensions of psychosocial development be added at the doctoral level? What impact do support structures have on doctoral students' psychosocial development? Do the types of psychosocial development experienced in specific disciplines differ according to different research modes? What impact does feedback at particular turning points have on psychosocial development?

Adult Development

How is the educational experience different at the doctoral level with regard to students' ego and intellectual development? How does the planned transition to doctoral education influence the student's identity? Are there more effective ways of teaching at the doctoral level that may be more beneficial to students' learning?

Social Identity Development

Who are doctoral students, and how do their previous educational experiences and backgrounds influence their identities throughout the doctoral experience? How do race, gender, sexual orientation, religion, ability, socioeconomic status, and age affect their development? How does the composition of departmental and institutional faculty and staff influence students' development, particularly those who are underrepresented from different sociocultural identities? How is the choice of research topic or the discipline affected by students' identity, and how do their identities factor into these choices? How does faculty identity development, particularly in relation to racial and gender identity development, affect their teaching and advising of doctoral students?

Cognitive-Structural Development

How do disciplinary and paradigmatic assumptions influence cognitive and epistemological development at the doctoral level? How does the research mode (independent versus collaborative) affect students' cognitive development? What is the effect of particular coursework experiences or assignments on their development in this area? Do different advising or teaching styles affect doctoral students' cognitive or epistemological development? Does part-time status have an effect on the nature of this development?

Professional Development

How does discipline affect the socialization process? How is socialization influenced by students' and faculty members' prior educational experiences? Does the socialization experience adequately prepare graduates entering the workforce? What is the impact of institutional and departmental culture on the socialization experience? How do students from underrepresented populations experience the socialization process?

Campus-Environment Dynamics

How does the campus influence the doctoral student's development? What effect do offices and student gathering spaces have on doctoral students' development and integration? How is the development of doctoral students affected by living in residence halls? How do different institutional environments affect doctoral students and their development?

Student Departure and Success

How are students of different sociocultural backgrounds affected by departure, and how do these characteristics influence the decision to depart? What impact do discipline, department, and institutional context have on the decision to depart a degree program? How do prior developmental experiences, or lack thereof, contribute to the decision to depart?

Conclusion

We are just beginning to understand the doctoral student. We have much to learn about this diverse population, their needs, their challenges, and their opportunities for support and success. The transitions these students experience and the role that their relationships play are unlike any others in their prior academic experiences. At the same time, the preparation doctoral students receive and its effects on them merit further exploration and understanding. We must remember that today's doctoral students are tomorrow's scholars, educators, researchers, and leaders and that high attrition among these students has social, economic, and personal ramifications for all of us. Through understanding the challenges of the doctoral program and providing the support to weather these challenges, we may all reap the benefits.

Appendix: Details of Research Conducted to Construct the Model

The model of doctoral student development used in this monograph results from several empirical studies focusing on doctoral student success and development. Interviews with 177 doctoral students in all phases of study were analyzed, encompassing individuals from various disciplines and institutions from across the United States. The following table presents an overview of these studies.

Purpose of Study and Citation	Year Conducted	Number of Students Interviewed	Disciplines	Number of Institutions
To explore the skills and habits of mind required to obtain a Ph.D. in education (Gardner, 2007)	2004	11	Counseling psychology, teaching and learning, educational psychology, higher education	1
To compare and contrast the experiences of doctoral students in two disciplines from two institutions (Gardner, 2007)	2004	40	Chemistry, history	2
To understand the dimensions of graduate student involvement (Gardner and Barnes, 2007)	2005	10	Higher education	5
To explore the development that occurs during doctoral education (Gardner, Vanek, Frugé, and Neider, 2006)	2006	12	Higher education	3
To contrast the experiences of doctoral students in departments with high and low completion rates (Gardner, forthcoming)	2006	60	Communications, English, oceanography, engineering, mathematics, psychology	1
To investigate the transition from full-time employment to full-time graduate student status (Gardner and McCoy, 2008)	2007	14	Higher education	4
To understand the experience of the first-generation doctoral student (Gardner, 2009)	2008	10	History, education, counseling, forestry, psychology	1

References

Abedi, J., and Benkin, E. (1987). The effects of students' academic, financial, and demographic variables on time to the doctorate. *Research in Higher Education, 27*(1), 3–14.

Aguinis, H., and others. (1996). Power bases of faculty supervisors and educational outcomes for graduate students. *Journal of Higher Education, 67*(3), 267–297.

American Council on Education. (1949). *The student personnel point of view.* Washington, DC: American Council on Education.

Antony, J. S. (2002). Reexamining doctoral student socialization and professional development: Moving beyond the congruence and assimilation orientation. *Higher Education: Handbook of Theory and Research* (Vol. XVII, pp. 349–380). New York: Agathon Press.

Austin, A. E. (2002). Preparing the next generation of faculty: Graduate school as socialization to the academic career. *Journal of Higher Education, 73,* 94–121.

Austin, A. E., and McDaniels, M. (2006). Preparing the professoriate of the future: Graduate student socialization for faculty roles. *Higher Education: Handbook of Theory and Research, 21,* 397–456.

Baird, L. L. (1972). The relation of graduate students' role relations to their stage of academic career, employment, and academic success. *Organizational Behavior and Human Performance, 7,* 428–441.

Baird, L. L. (1993). Using research and theoretical models of graduate student progress. In L. L. Baird (Ed.), *Increasing graduate student retention and degree attainment* (pp. 3–12). San Francisco: Jossey-Bass.

Baird, L. L. (1995). Helping graduate students: A graduate adviser's view. In A. S. Pruitt-Logan and P. D. Isaac (Eds.), *Student services for the changing graduate student population* (pp. 25–32). San Francisco: Jossey-Bass.

Baird, L. L. (1997). Completing the dissertation: Theory, research, and practice. In L. F. Goodchild, K. E. Green, E. L. Katz, and R. C. Kluever (Eds.), *Rethinking the dissertation process: Tackling personal and institutional obstacles* (pp. 99–105). San Francisco: Jossey-Bass.

Bargar, R. R., and Mayo-Chamberlain, J. (1983). Advisor and advisee issues in doctoral education. *Journal of Higher Education, 54,* 407–432.

Barker, S., Felstehausen, G., Couch, S., and Henry, J. (1997). Orientation programs for older and delayed-entry graduate students. *NASPA Journal, 35,* 57–68.

Barnes, B. J. (forthcoming). The nature of exemplary advisor's expectations and the ways they may influence doctoral persistence. *Journal of College Student Retention.*

Baxter Magolda, M. B. (1989). Gender differences in cognitive development: An analysis of cognitive complexity and learning styles. *Journal of College Student Development, 30,* 213–220.

Baxter Magolda, M. B. (1995). The integration of relational and impersonal knowing in young adults' epistemological development. *Journal of College Student Development, 36,* 205–216.

Baxter Magolda, M. B. (1996). Epistemological development in graduate and professional education. *Review of Higher Education, 19*(3), 283–304.

Baxter Magolda, M. B. (1998). Developing self-authorship in graduate school. In M. S. Anderson (Ed.), *The experience of being in graduate school: An exploration* (pp. 41–54). San Francisco: Jossey-Bass.

Becher, T. (1981). Towards a definition of disciplinary cultures. *Studies in Higher Education, 6,* 109–122.

Belenky, M. F., Clinchy, B. M., Goldberger, N. R., and Tarule, J. M. (1986). *Women's ways of knowing: The development of self, voice, and mind.* New York: Basic Books.

Berelson, B. (1960). *Graduate education in the United States.* New York: McGraw-Hill.

Berg, H. M., and Ferber, M. A. (1983). Men and women graduate students: Who succeeds and why? *Journal of Higher Education, 54*(6), 629–648.

Biglan, A. (1973). The characteristics of subject matter in different academic areas. *Journal of Applied Psychology, 57,* 195–203.

Bolker, J. (1998). *Writing your dissertation in fifteen minutes a day: A guide to starting, revising, and finishing your doctoral thesis.* New York: Owl Books.

Boote, D. N., & Beile, P. M. (2005). Scholars before researchers: On the centrality of the dissertation literature review in research preparation. *Educational Researcher, 34*(6), 3–15.

Bowen, W. G., and Rudenstine, N. L. (1992). *In pursuit of the Ph.D.* Princeton, NJ: Princeton University Press.

Boyle, P., and Boice, B. (1998). Best practices for enculturation: Collegiality, mentoring, and structure. In M. S. Anderson (Ed.), *The experience of being in graduate school: An exploration* (pp. 87–94). San Francisco: Jossey-Bass.

Braxton, J. M., and Hargens, L. L. (1996). Variation among academic disciplines: Analytical frameworks and research. *Higher Education: Handbook of Theory and Research* (Vol. 11, pp. 1–46).

Brown, H. A. (2005). *Graduate enrollment and degrees: 1986 to 2004.* Washington, DC: Council of Graduate Schools.

Brown, M. C., Davis, G. L., and McClendon, S. A. (1999). Mentoring graduate students of color: Myths, models, and modes. *Peabody Journal of Education, 74,* 105–118.

Brown-Wright, D. A., Dubick, R. A., and Newman, I. (1997). Graduate assistant expectation and faculty perception: Implications for mentoring and training. *Journal of College Student Development, 38*(4), 410–416.

Bryant, M. T. (2003). *The portable dissertation advisor.* Thousand Oaks, CA: Corwin Press.

Carnegie Foundation for the Advancement of Teaching. (2007). *Basic classification description.* Retrieved January 18, 2009, from http://www.carnegiefoundation.org/classifications/index.asp?key=791.

Cao, W. (2001, April). *How male and female doctoral students experience their doctoral programs similarly and differently.* Paper presented at the American Educational Research Association, Seattle, WA.

Cass, V. C. (1979). Homosexual identity formation: A theoretical model. *Journal of Homosexuality, 4,* 219–235.

Castellanos, J., Gloria, A. M., and Kamimura, M. (Eds.). (2006). *The Latina/o pathway to the Ph.D.: Abriendo caminos.* Sterling, VA: Stylus.

Chickering, A. W., and Havighurst, R. J. (1981). The life cycle. In A. W. Chickering (Ed.), *The modern American college* (pp. 16–50). San Francisco: Jossey-Bass.

Chickering, A. W., McDowell, J., and Campagna, D. (1969). Institutional differences and student development. *Journal of Educational Psychology, 60*(4), 315–326.

Chickering, A. W., and Reisser, L. (1993). *Education and identity* (2nd ed.). San Francisco: Jossey-Bass.

Choy, S. P., and Cataldi, E. F. (2006). *Student financing of graduate and first-professional education, 2003–04.* NCES 2006–185. Washington, DC: National Center for Education Statistics.

Clark, B. R. (1987). *The academic life: Small worlds, different worlds.* Princeton, NJ: The Carnegie Foundation.

Clark, S. M., and Corcoran, M. (1986). Perspectives on the professional socialization of women faculty: A case of accumulative disadvantage? *Journal of Higher Education, 57,* 20–43.

Cook, M. M., and Swanson, A. (1978). The interaction of student and program variables for the purpose of developing a model for predicting graduation from graduate programs over a ten-year period. *Research in Higher Education, 8,* 83–91.

Council of Graduate Schools. (1995). *Research student and supervisor: An approach to good supervisory practice.* Washington, DC: Council of Graduate Schools.

Council of Graduate Schools. (2004). *Organization and administration of graduate education.* Washington, DC: Council of Graduate Schools.

Council of Graduate Schools. (2005). *The doctor of philosophy degree: A policy statement.* Washington, DC: Council of Graduate Schools.

Council of Graduate Schools. (2008). *Ph.D. completion and attrition: Analysis of baseline program data from the Ph.D. completion project.* Washington, DC: Council of Graduate Schools.

Council on Postsecondary Education. (2007). *Kentucky's STEM imperative: Competing in the global economy.* Louisville: University of Kentucky.

Crosby, G. A. (1996). Graduate programs in chemistry: A time for innovation and reform. [commentary]. *Journal of Chemical Education, 73*(10), A235.

Cross, W. E., Jr. (1971). Toward a psychology of black liberation: The Negro-to-black conversion experience. *Black World, 20*(9), 13–27.

Cross, W. T. (1996). Pathway to the professoriate: The American Indian faculty pipeline. In C. Turner, M. Garcia, A. Nora, and L. I. Rendon (Eds.), *Racial and ethnic diversity in higher education* (pp. 327–336). Boston: Pearson Custom Publishing.

Davis, A. P., and McCuen, R. H. (1995). Part-time graduate education: Obstacles, conflicts, and suggestions. *Journal of Professional Issues in Engineering Education and Practice, 121*(2), 108–113.

Delamont, S., Atkinson, P., and Parry, O. (2000). *The doctoral experience: Success and failure in graduate school.* London: Falmer Press.

Downing, N. E., and Roush, K. L. (1985). From passive acceptance to active commitment: A model of feminist identity development for women. *Counseling Psychologist, 13,* 695–709.

Duncan, B. L. (1976). Minority students. In E. L. Katz and R. T. Hartnett (Eds.), *Scholars in the making: The development of graduate and professional students.* Cambridge, MA: Ballinger.

Dziech, B. W., and Weiner, L. (1990). *The lecherous professor: Sexual harassment on campus* (2nd ed.). Urbana: University of Illinois Press.

Egan, J. M. (1989). Graduate school and the self: A theoretical view of some negative effects of professional socialization. *Teaching Sociology, 17,* 200–208.

Elkana, Y. (2006). Unmasking uncertainties and embracing contradictions: Graduate education in the sciences. In C. M. Golde and G. E. Walker (Eds.), *Envisioning the future of doctoral education: Preparing stewards of the discipline* (pp. 65–96). San Francisco: Jossey-Bass.

Ellis, E. M. (2001). The impact of race and gender on graduate school socialization, satisfaction with doctoral study, and commitment to degree completion. *Western Journal of Black Studies, 25,* 30–45.

Erikson, E. H. (1959). *Identity and the life cycle.* New York: International Universities Press.

Ethington, C. A., and Pisani, A. (1993). The RA and TA experience: Impediments and benefits to graduate study. *Research in Higher Education, 34*(3), 343–354.

Evans, N. J., Forney, D. S., and Guido-DiBrito, F. (1998). *Student development in college: Theory, research, and practice.* San Francisco: Jossey-Bass.

Ferrer de Valero, Y. (2001). Departmental factors effecting time-to-degree and completion rates of doctoral students at one land grant research institution. *Journal of Higher Education, 72,* 341–367.

Fischer, B. A., and Zigmond, M. J. (1998). Survival skills for graduate school and beyond. In M. S. Anderson (Ed.), *The experience of being in graduate school: An exploration* (pp. 29–40). San Francisco: Jossey-Bass.

Forney, D. S., and Davis, T. L. (2002). Ongoing transition sessions for student affairs master's students. *Journal of College Student Development, 43*(2), 288–293.

Fox, M. F. (2001). Women, science, and academia: Graduate education and careers. *Gender and Society, 15*(5), 654–666.

Gaff, J. G. (2002). The disconnect between graduate education and faculty realities. *Liberal Education, 88*(3), 6.

Gardner, S. K. (2005). "If it were easy, everyone would have a Ph.D." Doctoral student success: Socialization and disciplinary perspectives. Unpublished doctoral dissertation, Washington State University.

Gardner, S. K. (2007). "I heard it through the grapevine": Doctoral student socialization in chemistry and history. *Higher Education, 54,* 723–740.

Gardner, S. K. (2008a, November). *Contrasting the socialization experiences of doctoral students in high- and low-completing departments: A qualitative analysis of disciplinary and institutional contexts.* Paper presented at an annual meeting of the Association for the Study of Higher Education, Jacksonville, FL.

Gardner, S. K. (2008b). Fitting the mold of graduate school. *Innovative Higher Education, 33,* 125–138.

Gardner, S. K. (2008c). "What's too much and what's too little?" The process of becoming an independent researcher in doctoral education. *Journal of Higher Education, 79,* 326–350.

Gardner, S. K. (2009). Understanding the experience of the first-generation doctoral student. Unpublished manuscript.

Gardner, S. K. (forthcoming). Contrasting the socialization experiences of doctoral students in high- and low-completing departments: A qualitative analysis of disciplinary and institutional context. *Journal of Higher Education.*

Gardner, S. K., and Barnes, B. J. (2007). Graduate student involvement: Socialization for the professional role. *Journal of College Student Development, 48,* 369–387.

Gardner, S. K., Hayes, M. T., and Neider, X. (2007). The dispositions and skills of a Ph.D. in education: Perspectives of faculty and graduate students in one college of education. *Innovative Higher Education, 31*(5), 287–299.

Gardner, S. K., and McCoy, D. (2008, November). *The transition from full-time employment to full-time graduate student.* Paper presented at an annual meeting of the Association for the Study of Higher Education, Jacksonville, FL.

Gardner, S. K., Vanek, G. T., Frugé, C., and Neider, X. (2006). The Ph.D. as journey: A qualitative exploration of development in doctoral education. Unpublished manuscript.

Gay, G. (2004). Navigating marginality en route to the professoriate: Graduate students of color learning and living in academia. *International Journal of Qualitative Studies in Education, 17*(2), 265–288.

Gilligan, C. (1978). *In a different voice: Psychological theory and women's development.* Cambridge, MA: Harvard University Press.

Girves, J. E., and Wemmerus, V. (1988). Developing models of graduate student degree progress. *Journal of Higher Education, 59*(2), 163–189.

Golde, C. M. (1998). Beginning graduate school: Explaining first-year doctoral attrition. In M. S. Anderson (Ed.), *The experience of being in graduate school: An exploration* (pp. 55–64). San Francisco: Jossey-Bass.

Golde, C. M. (1999). After the offer, before the deal: Negotiating a first academic job. *Academe, 85*(1), 44–50.

Golde, C. M. (2005). The role of the department and discipline in doctoral student attrition: Lessons from four departments. *Journal of Higher Education, 76,* 669–700.

Golde, C. M., and Dore, T. M. (2001). *At cross purposes: What the experiences of doctoral students reveal about doctoral education.* Retrieved January 24, 2008, from http://www.phd-survey.org.

Golde, C. M., and Walker, G. E. (Eds.). (2006). *Envisioning the future of doctoral education: Preparing stewards of the discipline.* San Francisco: Jossey-Bass.

Gonzalez, J. C. (2006). Academic socialization experiences of Latina doctoral students: A qualitative understanding of support systems that aid and challenges that hinder the process. *Journal of Hispanic Higher Education, 5*(4), 347–365.

Gonzalez, K. P., and Marin, P. (2002). Inside doctoral education in America: Voices of Latinas/os in pursuit of the PhD. *Journal of College Student Development, 43,* 540–557.

Goodchild, L. F., Green, K. E., Katz, E. L., and Kluever, R. C. (Eds.). (1997). *Rethinking the dissertation process: Tackling personal and institutional obstacles.* San Francisco: Jossey-Bass.

Goodman, J., Schlossberg, N. K., and Anderson, M. L. (2006). *Counseling adults in transition: Linking practice with theory* (3rd ed.). New York: Springer.

Grant-Vallone, E. J., and Ensher, E. A. (2000). Effects of peer mentoring on types of mentor support, program satisfaction and graduate student stress: A dyadic perspective. *Journal of College Student Development, 41*(6), 637–642.

Green, A. L., and Scott, L. V. (Eds.). (2003). *Journey to the Ph.D.: How to navigate the process as African Americans.* Sterling, VA: Stylus.

Green, K. E. (1997). Psychosocial factors affecting dissertation completion. In L. F. Goodchild, K. E. Green, E. L. Katz, and R. C. Kluever (Eds.), *Rethinking the dissertation process: Tackling personal and institutional obstacles* (pp. 57–64). San Francisco: Jossey-Bass.

Gumport, P. J. (1993). Graduate education and organized research in the United States. In B. R. Clark (Ed.), *The research foundations of graduate education: Germany, Britain, France, United States, Japan* (pp. 225–260). Berkeley: University of California Press.

Harper, W. R. (1905). *The trend in higher education.* Chicago: University of Chicago Press.

Hartnett, R. T. (1976). Environments for advanced learning. In J. Katz and R. T. Hartnett (Eds.), *Scholars in the making: The development of graduate and professional students.* Cambridge, MA: Ballinger.

Hartnett, R. T. (1981). Sex differences in the environments of graduate students and faculty. *Research in Higher Education, 14*(3), 211–227.

Heinrich, K. T. (1995). Doctoral advisement relationships between women: On friendship and betrayal. *Journal of Higher Education, 66*(4), 447–469.

Heiss, A. M. (1970). *Challenges to graduate schools.* San Francisco: Jossey-Bass.

Helms, J. E., and Cook, D. A. (2005). Models of oppression and sociorace. In M. E. Wilson and L. E. Wolf-Wendel (Eds.), *ASHE reader on college student development theory* (pp. 235–258). Boston: Pearson Custom Publishing.

Herzig, A. H. (2004a). Becoming mathematicians: Women and students of color choosing and leaving doctoral mathematics. *Review of Educational Research, 74*(2), 171–214.

Herzig, A. H. (2004b). "Slaughtering this beautiful math": Graduate women choosing and leaving mathematics. *Gender and Education, 16*(3), 379–395.

Hoare, C. (2006). Growing a discipline at the borders of thought. In C. Hoare (Ed.), *Handbook of adult development and learning* (pp. 3–26). New York: Oxford University Press.

Hoffer, T. B., and others. (2002). *Doctorate recipients from United States universities: Summary report 2002*. Chicago: National Opinion Research Center.

Hoffer, T. B., and others. (2004). *Doctorate recipients from United States universities: Summary report 2003*. Chicago: National Opinion Research Center.

Hoffer, T. B., and others. (2005). *Doctorate recipients from United States universities: Summary report 2004*. Chicago: National Opinion Research Center.

Hoffer, T. B., and others. (2006). *Doctorate recipients from United States universities: Summary report 2005*. Chicago: National Opinion Research Center.

Holberg, J. L., and Taylor, M. M. (1996). Apprenticeship versus partnership: Graduate students as administrators. *Composition Chronicle: A Newsletter for Writing Teachers, 8*(9), 6–8.

Isaac, P. D., Quinlan, S. V., and Walker, M. M. (1992). Faculty perceptions of the doctoral dissertation. *The Journal of Higher Education, 63*(3), 241–268.

John, W. C. (1934). *Graduate study in universities and colleges in the United States*. Washington, DC: Office of Education, U.S. Department of the Interior.

Jones, E. (2003). Beyond supply and demand: Assessing the Ph.D. job market. *Occupational Outlook Quarterly, 46*(4), 22–33.

Josselson, R. (1973). Psychodynamic aspects of identity formation in college women. *Journal of Youth and Adolescence, 2*, 3–52.

Katz, E. L. (1997). Key players in the dissertation process. In L. F. Goodchild, K. E. Green, E. L. Katz, and R. C. Kluever (Eds.), *Rethinking the dissertation process: Tackling personal and institutional obstacles* (pp. 5–16). San Francisco: Jossey-Bass.

Katz, J. (1976). Development of the mind. In J. Katz and R. T. Hartnett (Eds.), *Scholars in the making: The development of graduate and professional students* (pp. 107–126). Cambridge, MA: Ballinger.

Katz, J., and Hartnett, R. T. (Eds.). (1976). *Scholars in the making: The development of graduate and professional students*. Cambridge, MA: Ballinger.

King, M. F. (2003). *On the right track: A manual for research mentors*. Washington, DC: Council of Graduate Schools.

King, P. M. (1994). Theories of college student development: Sequences and consequences. *Journal of College Student Development, 35*, 413–421.

King, P. M., & Kitchener, K. S. (1994). *Developing reflective judgment: Understanding and promoting intellectual growth and critical thinking in adolescents and adults*. San Francisco: Jossey-Bass.

Knefelkamp, L., Widick, C., and Parker, C. A. (1978). *Applying new developmental findings*. San Francisco: Jossey-Bass.

Kniffin, K. M. (2007). Accessibility to the Ph.D. and professoriate for first-generation college graduates: Review and implications for students, faculty, and campus policies. *American Academic, 3*, 49–79.

Knowles, M. F., and Harleston, B. W. (1997). *Achieving diversity in the professoriate: Challenges and opportunities*. New York: American Council on Education.

Kohlberg, L. (1975). The cognitive-developmental approach to moral education. *Phi Delta Kappan, 56*, 670–677.

Komives, S. R., and Taub, D. J. (2000). Advancing professionally through doctoral education. In M. J. Barr and M. K. Desler (Eds.), *The handbook of student affairs administration* (2nd ed., pp. 508–534). San Francisco: Jossey-Bass.

Korinek, K., Howard, J. A., and Bridges, G. S. (1999). "Train the whole scholar": A developmentally based program for teaching assistant training in sociology. *Teaching Sociology, 27*(4), 343–359.

Kuh, C. V. (1996). Is there a Ph.D. glut? Is that the right question? *CGS Communicator,* 1–4.

Kuh, G. D., and Thomas, M. L. (1983). The use of adult development theory with graduate students. *Journal of College Student Personnel, 24*(1), 12–19.

LaPidus, J. B. (1997, November 14). Why pursuing a Ph.D. is risky business. *Chronicle of Higher Education,* A60.

Larke, P. J., Patitu, C. L., Webb-Johnson, G., and Young-Hawkins, L. (1999). Embracing minority graduate students: The mentoring approach. *NASPA Journal, 2*(1), 47–55.

Lau, L. K. (2003). Institutional factors affecting student retention. *Education, 124,* 126–136.

Lave, J., and Wenger, E. (1991). *Situated learning: Legitimate peripheral participation.* New York: Cambridge University Press.

Le, T., and Gardner, S. K. (2007, November). *Understanding the doctoral experience of Asian international students in the STEM fields: An exploration of one institutional context.* Paper presented at an annual meeting of the Association for the Study of Higher Education, Louisville, KY.

Lenz, K. S. (1997). Nontraditional-aged women and the dissertation: A case study approach. In L. F. Goodchild, K. E. Green, E. L. Katz, and R. C. Kluever (Eds.), *Rethinking the dissertation process: Tackling personal and institutional obstacles* (pp. 65–74). San Francisco: Jossey-Bass.

Levinson, D. J. (1990). A theory of life structure development in adulthood. In C. N. Alexander and E. J. Langer (Eds.), *Higher stages of human development: Perspectives on adult growth* (pp. 35–53). New York: Oxford University Press.

Lott, J., and Gardner, S. K. (forthcoming). Doctoral student attrition in the STEM fields: An exploration of event history analysis. *Journal of College Student Retention.*

Lovitts, B. E. (2001). *Leaving the ivory tower: The causes and consequences of departure from doctoral study.* Lanham, MD: Rowman & Littlefield.

Lovitts, B. E. (2005). Being a good course-taker is not enough: A theoretical perspective on the transition to independent research. *Studies in Higher Education, 30,* 137–154.

Lovitts, B. E. (2007). *Making the implicit explicit: Creating performance expectations for the dissertation.* Sterling, VA: Stylus.

Lovitts, B. E. (2008). The transition to independent research: Who makes it, who doesn't, and why. *Journal of Higher Education, 79,* 296–325.

Lucas, C. J. (1994). *American higher education: A history.* New York: St. Martin's Griffin.

MacLachlan, A. J. (2006). *Developing graduate students of color for the professoriate in science, technology, engineering, and mathematics.* Berkeley, CA: Center for Studies in Higher Education.

Maher, M. A., Ford, M. E., and Thompson, C. M. (2004). Degree progress of women doctoral students: Factors that constrain, facilitate, and differentiate. *Review of Higher Education, 27*(3), 385–408.

Malaney, G. D. (1988). Graduate education as an area of research in the field of higher education. *Higher Education: Handbook of Theory and Research, 4,* 397–454.

Margolis, E., and Romero, M. (1998). "The department is very male, very white, very old, and very conservative": The functioning of the hidden curriculum in graduate sociology departments. *Harvard Educational Review, 68,* 1–32.

McEwen, M. K. (2003). The nature and uses of theory. In S. R. Komives and D. B. Woodard (Eds.), *Student services: A handbook for the profession* (pp. 153–178). San Francisco: Jossey-Bass.

McEwen, M. K. (2005). The nature and uses of theory. In M. E. Wilson and L. Wolf-Wendel (Eds.), *ASHE reader on college student development theory* (pp. 5–24). Boston: Pearson Custom Publishing.

Mendoza, P. (2007). Academic capitalism and doctoral student socialization: A case study. *Journal of Higher Education, 78*(1), 71–96.

Merriam, S. B. (1984). Adult development: Implications for adult education. In S. B. Merriam (Ed.), *The new update on adult learning theory: New directions for adult and continuing education* (pp. 3–13). San Francisco: Jossey-Bass.

Merriam, S. B., and Clark, M. C. (2006). Learning and development: The connection in adulthood. In C. Hoare (Ed.), *Handbook of adult development and learning* (pp. 27–51). Oxford, UK: Oxford University Press.

Merton, R. K. (1957). *Social theory and social structure.* New York: Free Press.

National Center for Education Statistics. (2003). *NCES Fast Facts.* Retrieved December 3, 2003, from http://nces.ed.gov/fastfacts.

National Research Council (2001). *From scarcity to visibility: Gender differences in the careers of doctoral scientists and engineers.* Washington, DC: National Academy Press.

National Science Board. (2008). *Science and engineering indicators, 2008.* Arlington, VA: National Science Foundation.

National Science Foundation. (2004a). *Alliances for graduate education and the professoriate.* Retrieved February 26, 2006, from http://www.nsf.gov/pubs/2004/nsf04575/nsf04575.htm.

National Science Foundation. (2004b). *Science and engineering degrees, by race/ethnicity of recipients: 1992–2001.* Arlington, VA: Division of Science Resources Statistics, National Science Foundation.

National Science Foundation (2006). *U.S. doctorates in the 20th century (NSF 06–319).* Washington, DC: National Science Foundation.

Nerad, M., June, R., and Miller, D. S. (Eds.). (1997). *Graduate education in the United States.* New York: Garland Publishing.

Nerad, M., and Miller, D. S. (1996). Increasing student retention in graduate and professional programs. In J. G. Haworth (Ed.), *Assessing graduate and professional education: Current realities, future prospects* (pp. 61–76). San Francisco: Jossey-Bass.

Nerad, M., and Miller, D. S. (1997). The institution cares: Berkeley's efforts to support dissertation writing in the humanities and social sciences. In L. F. Goodchild, K. E. Green, E. L. Katz, and R. C. Klueger (Eds.), *Rethinking the dissertation process: Tackling personal and institutional obstacles* (pp. 75–90). San Francisco: Jossey-Bass.

Nettles, M. T. (1990). Success in doctoral programs: Experiences of minority and white students. *American Journal of Education, 98*(4), 494–522.

Nettles, M. T., and Millett, C. M. (2006). *Three magic letters: Getting to Ph.D.* Baltimore: Johns Hopkins University Press.

Noble, K. A. (1994). *Changing doctoral degrees: An international perspective.* Suffolk, Great Britain: Edmundsbury Press.

Nyquist, J., and others. (1999). On the road to becoming a professor: The graduate student experience. *Change,* 18–27.

Nyquist, J., and Wulff, D. H. (1996). *Working effectively with graduate assistants.* Thousand Oaks, CA: Sage.

Osguthorpe, R. T., and Wong, M. J. (1993). The Ph.D. versus the Ed.D.: Time for a decision. *Innovative Higher Education, 18,* 47–63.

Owen, T. R. (1999). Self-directed learning readiness among graduate students: Implications for orientation programs. *Journal of College Student Development, 40*(6), 739–743.

Pallas, A. M. (2001). Preparing education doctoral students for epistemological diversity. *Educational Researcher, 30*(5), 6–11.

Pascarella, E. T., and Terenzini, P. T. (2005). *How college affects students* (Vol. 2). San Francisco: Jossey-Bass.

Perna, L. W., and Hodgins, C. (1996, November). *The graduate assistantship: Facilitator of graduate students' professional socialization.* Paper presented at the Association for the Study of Higher Education, Memphis, TN.

Perry, W. G., Jr. (1968). *Forms of intellectual and ethical development in the college years: A scheme.* New York: Holt, Rinehart & Winston.

Peters, R. L. (1997). *Getting what you came for: The smart student's guide to earning a master's or Ph.D.* New York: Farrar, Straus & Giroux.

Phinney, J. S. (1989). Stages of ethnic identity development in minority group adolescents. *Journal of Early Adolescence, 9,* 34–39.

Piaget, J. (1952). *The origins of intelligence in children.* New York: International Universities Press.

Planty, M., and others. (2008). *The Condition of Education 2008.* Washington, DC: National Center for Education Statistics, U.S. Department of Education.

Price, J. (2006). Does a spouse slow you down?: Marriage and graduate student outcomes. Unpublished manuscript.

Rentz, T. (2003). The role of mentorship in developing African American students and professionals within the academy. In A. L. Green and L. V. Scott (Eds.), *Journey to the Ph.D.: How to navigate the process as African Americans* (pp. 225–236). Sterling, VA: Stylus.

Rodgers, R. F. (1990). Recent theories and research underlying student development. In D. Creamer and Associates (Eds.), *College student development: Theory and practice for the 1990s* (pp. 27–79). Alexandria, VA: American College Personnel Association.

Rosen, B. C., and Bates, A. P. (1967). The structure of socialization in graduate school. *Sociological Inquiry, 37,* 71–84.

Rosenblatt, H. S., and Christensen, C. (1993). "Welcome to the whole family": A graduate student orientation. *College Student Journal, 27*(4), 502–505.

Rossman, M. H. (2002). *Negotiating graduate school: A guide for graduate students.* Thousand Oaks, CA: Sage.

Sanford, N. (1962). *The American college.* New York: Wiley.

Sanford, N. (1966). *Self and society: Social change and individual development.* New York: Atherton Press.

Schroeder, D. S., and Mynatt, C. R. (1993). Female graduate students' perceptions of their interactions with male and female major professors. *Journal of Higher Education, 64*(5), 555–573.

Shulman, L. S., Golde, C. M., Conklin Bueschel, A., and Garabedian, K. J. (2006). Reclaiming education's doctorates: A critique and a proposal. *Educational Researcher, 35*(3), 25–32.

Smallwood, S. (2004, January 16). Doctor dropout. *Chronicle of Higher Education,* p. 19A.

Sodowsky, G. R., and others. (1994). World reviews of white American, mainland Chinese, Taiwanese, and African students: An investigation into between-group differences. *Journal of Cross-Cultural Psychology, 25*(3), 309–325.

Sorenson, G., and Kagan, D. (1967). Conflicts between doctoral candidates and their sponsors: A contrast in expectations. *Journal of Higher Education, 38*(1), 17–24.

Soto Antony, J., and Taylor, E. (2004). Theories and strategies of academic career socialization: Improving paths to the professoriate for black graduate students. In D. H. Wulff and A. E. Austin (Eds.), *Paths to the professoriate: Strategies for enriching the preparation of future faculty* (pp. 92–114). San Francisco: Jossey-Bass.

Strange, C. (1994). Student development: The evolution and status of an essential idea. *Journal of College Student Development, 35,* 399–412.

Strange, C. (2005). Student development: The evolution and status of an essential idea. In M. E. Wilson and L. Wolf-Wendel (Eds.), *ASHE reader on college student development theory* (pp. 25–41). Boston: Pearson Custom Publishing.

Syverson, P. D. (1999). Part-time study plus full-time employment: The new way to go to graduate school. *Education Statistics Quarterly, 1*(3), 13–15.

Taub, D. J., and Komives, S. R. (1998). A comprehensive graduate orientation program: Practicing what we preach. *Journal of College Student Development, 39*(4), 394–398.

Tennant, M., and Pogson, P. (2002). *Learning and change in the adult years: A developmental perspective.* San Francisco: Jossey-Bass.

Thelin, J. R. (2004). *A history of American higher education.* Baltimore: Johns Hopkins University Press.

Tierney, W. G., and Bensimon, E. M. (1996). *Promotion and tenure: Community and socialization in academe.* Albany: State University of New York Press.

Tierney, W. G., and Rhoads, R. A. (1994). *Enhancing promotion, tenure and beyond: Faculty socialization as a cultural process.* Washington, DC: George Washington University.

Tinto, V. (1993). *Leaving college: Rethinking the causes and cures of student attrition.* (2nd ed.). Chicago: University of Chicago Press.

Toma, J. D. (2002, November). *Legitimacy, differentiation, and the promise of the Ed.D. in higher education.* Paper presented at the Association for the Study of Higher Education, Sacramento, CA.

Trower, C. A., and Chait, R. P. (2002, March/April). Faculty diversity: Too little for too long. *Harvard Magazine,* 33–37.

Turner, C.S.V. (2002). *Diversifying the faculty: A guidebook for search committees.* Washington, DC: Association of American Colleges and Universities.

Turner, C.S.V., and Thompson, J. R. (1993). Socializing women doctoral students: Minority and majority experiences. *Review of Higher Education, 16,* 355–370.

U.S. Department of Education. (2002). *Integrated postsecondary education data system fall enrollment survey.* Washington, DC: National Center for Education Statistics.

U.S. Department of Education and National Center for Education Statistics. (1999). *Students with disabilities in postsecondary education: A profile of preparation, participation, and outcomes.* Washington, DC: National Center for Education Statistics.

University of Chicago. (2002). *Skills identification for PhD students and postdocs.* Chicago: University of Chicago Press.

Van Maanen, J. (1984). Doing new things in old ways: The chains of socialization. In J. L. Bess (Ed.), *College and university organization: Insights from the behavioral sciences* (pp. 211–247). New York: New York University Press.

Vickio, C. J., and Tack, M. W. (1989). Orientation programming for graduate students: An institutional imperative. *NACADA Journal, 9*(2), 37–42.

Vlisides, D., and Eddy, J. (1993). Graduate student orientation models. *College Student Journal, 27*(1), 96–98.

Walker, G. E., and others. (2008). *The formation of scholars: Rethinking doctoral education for the twenty-first century.* San Francisco: Jossey-Bass.

Weathersby, R. P. (1981). Ego development. In A. W. Chickering (Ed.), *The modern American college* (pp. 51–75). San Francisco: Jossey-Bass.

Weidman, J. C., and Stein, E. L. (2003). Socialization of doctoral students to academic norms. *Research in Higher Education, 44,* 641–656.

Weidman, J. C., Twale, D. J., and Stein, E. L. (2001). *Socialization of graduate and professional students in higher education: A perilous passage?* San Francisco: Jossey-Bass.

Wilson, M. E., and Wolf-Wendel, L. E. (Eds.). (2005). *ASHE reader on college student development theory.* Boston: Pearson Custom Publishing.

Wilson, R. (2004, December 3). Where the elite teach, it's still a man's world. *Chronicle of Higher Education,* p. A8.

Zachary, L. (2000). *The mentor's guide: Facilitating effective learning relationships.* San Francisco: Jossey-Bass.

Zhao, C.-M., Golde, C. M., and McCormick, A. C. (2005, April). *More than a signature: How advisor choice and advisor behavior affect doctoral student satisfaction.* Paper presented at the annual meeting of the American Educational Research Association, Montreal, Quebec.

Name Index

A
Abedi, J., 6, 31, 68
Aguinis, H., 6, 58, 68, 69
Anderson, M. L., 43, 45, 54, 78, 82
Antony, J. S., 6
Atkinson, P., 63
Austin, A. E., 6, 57, 73, 99

B
Baird, L. L., 6, 11, 66, 68
Bargar, R. R., 6, 66, 68, 97
Barker, S., 36, 45
Barnes, B. J., 68, 73, 74, 99, 106
Bates, A. P., 6
Baxter Magolda, M. B., 50, 94, 98
Becher, T., 38
Beile, P. M., 6
Belenky, M. F., 17, 28, 50, 57, 69
Benkin, E., 6, 31, 68
Bensimon, E. M., 70
Berelson, B., 31, 33, 36, 37, 66
Berg, H. M., 34
Biglan, A., 38
Boice, B., 58, 95
Bolker, J., 80
Boote, D. N., 6
Bowen, W. G., 2, 6, 11, 31, 45, 59, 74, 80, 87, 88
Boyle, P, 58, 95
Braxton, J. M., 38
Bridges, G. S., 95
Brown, H. A., 36

Brown, M. C., 35, 70, 96
Brown-Wright, D. A., 73, 95
Bryant, M. T., 80

C
Campagna, D., 16, 19, 24
Cao, W., 6
Cass, V. C., 16, 26
Castellanos, J., 35
Cataldi, E. F., 33, 35
Chait, R. P., 96
Chickering, A. W., 16, 17, 19, 20, 21, 22, 24, 46, 47, 48, 49, 54, 55, 58, 63, 65, 66, 69, 71, 74, 81, 83, 84, 95, 96
Choy, S. P., 33, 35
Christensen, C., 45
Clark, B. R., 6, 7, 11, 34, 38, 51, 54, 57, 65, 68, 69
Clinchy, B. M., 17, 28, 50, 57, 69
Conklin Bueschel, A., 30
Cook, D. A., 11, 24, 25, 26
Corcoran, M., 6, 34, 57, 68, 69
Couch, S., 36, 45
Crosby, G. A., 6
Cross, W. E., Jr., 16
Cross, W. T., 3

D
Davis, A. P., 35, 40, 45, 70, 95, 96
Delamont, S., 63
Dore, T. M., 11
Downing, N. E., 26

Komives, S. R., 1, 45
Korinek, K., 95
Kuh, C. V., 84
Kuh, G. D., 7

L

LaPidus, J. B., 84
Larke, P. J., 35, 70, 96
Lau, L. K., 2
Lave, J., 51
Le, T., 35
Lenz, K. S., 36
Levinson, D. J., 7, 22, 49
Lott, J., 6, 45, 59
Lovitts, B. E., 2, 3, 6, 11, 41, 44, 45, 54,
    57, 58, 59, 60, 63, 68, 74, 75, 79, 80,
    81, 82, 87, 88, 100
Lucas, C. J., 33, 34

M

MacLachlan, A. J., 70
Maher, M. A., 6, 34
Malaney, G. D., 31
Margolis, E., 6, 34, 95
Marin, P., 6
Mayo-Chamberlain, J., 6, 66, 68, 97
McClendon, S. A., 35, 70, 96
McCormick, A. C., 68
McCoy, D., 43, 106
McCuen, R. H., 40, 95
McDaniels, M., 57, 73
McDowell, J., 16, 19, 24
McEwen, M. K., 2, 15, 17, 22, 24, 102
Mendoza, P., 6
Merriam, S. B., 7, 11, 51, 54, 65
Merton, R. K., 21
Miller, D. S., 6, 11, 31, 80, 94, 100
Millett, C. M., 3, 11, 31, 37, 68
Mynatt, C. R., 6, 34, 69, 83

N

Neider, X., 63, 106
Nerad, M., 6, 11, 31, 80, 94, 100
Nettles, M. T., 3, 11, 31, 35, 37, 68
Newman, I., 73, 95

Noble, K. A., 5, 31
Nyquist, J., 40, 55, 73, 95, 99

O

Osguthorpe, R. T., 30
Owen, T. R., 45

P

Pallas, A. M., 94
Parker, C. A., 5, 17
Parry, O., 63
Pascarella, E. T., 4, 45, 50
Patitu, C. L., 35, 70, 96
Perna, L. W., 73
Perry, W. G., Jr., 16, 27, 28, 50, 55, 57, 63
Peters, R. L., 98
Phinney, J. S., 26
Piaget, J., 17, 26, 27, 28
Pisani, A., 40, 73, 95
Planty, M., 2
Pogson, P., 51
Price, J., 37

Q

Quinlan, S. V., 6

R

Reisser, L., 17, 19, 20, 22, 46, 47, 48, 49,
    54, 55, 58, 63, 65, 66, 69, 71, 74, 81,
    83, 84, 95, 96
Rentz, T., 58
Rhoads, R. A., 21
Rodgers, R. F., 1, 12, 15
Romero, M., 6, 34, 95
Rosen, B. C., 6
Rosenblatt, H. S., 45
Rossman, M. H., 98
Roush, K. L., 26
Rudenstine, N. L., 2, 6, 11, 31, 45, 59, 74,
    80, 87, 88

S

Sanford, N., 7, 15, 16, 26
Schlossberg, N. K., 43, 45, 54, 78, 82
Schroeder, D. S., 6, 34, 69, 83

Scott, L. V., 6
Shulman, L. S., 30
Smallwood, S., 3
Sodowsky, G. R., 35
Sorenson, G., 68
Soto Antony, J., 6, 35, 95
Stein, E. L., 6, 41, 57, 72, 78, 79, 80, 81,
  83, 84, 85, 86, 93, 97
Strange, C., 12, 16
Swanson, A., 11
Syverson, P. D., 36

T

Tack, M. W., 45
Tarule, J. M., 17, 28, 50, 57, 69
Taub, D. J., 1, 45
Taylor, E., 6, 35, 95
Tennant, M., 51
Terenzini, P. T., 4, 45, 50
Thelin, J. R., 31, 32
Thomas, M. L., 7
Thompson, C. M., 6, 34
Tierney, W. G., 21, 70
Tinto, V., 46, 56, 58, 68, 83, 85, 93, 97
Toma, J. D., 30
Trower, C. A., 96
Turner, C. S. V., 6, 34, 96
Twale, D. J., 6, 41, 72, 78, 79, 80, 81, 83,
  84, 85, 86, 93, 97

V

Van Maanen, J., 43
Vanek, G. T., 106
Vickio, C. J., 45
Vlisides, D., 45

W

Walker, G. E., 2, 6, 7, 31, 32, 33, 39, 71,
  86, 93, 94, 97, 98, 99, 100
Weathersby, R. P., 50, 81, 83, 84
Webb-Johnson, G., 35, 70, 96
Weidman, J. C., 6, 41, 57, 72, 78, 79, 80,
  81, 83, 84, 85, 86, 93, 97
Weiner, L., 69
Wemmerus, V., 11, 68
Wenger, E., 51
Widick, C., 5, 17
Wilson, M. E., 24, 27, 33
Wolf-Wendel, L. E., 24, 27
Wong, M. J., 30
Wulff, D. H., 40, 55, 73, 95, 99

Y

Young-Hawkins, L., 35, 70, 96

Z

Zachary, L., 58
Zhao, C.-M., 68
Zigmond M. J., 69, 97

Subject Index

A

Adolescent stage of development, 19
Adult development, 22–23, 51, 89, 102
Advisor relationships, 66–70, 97–98
African American students, 34
African Americans, 33
American Council on Education, 1
Anticipatory socialization, 21, 41, 80
Asian American students, 34
Assistantships, 3, 39–40, 94–95
Attrition rates, 2–4. *See also* departures
Autonomy, 20
Awareness, integrated, 25–26

B

Balance, 48–49, 95

C

Campus-environment dynamics, 103
Candidacy. *See* development model
Candidacy phase. *See* Phase III: Candidacy
Career (professional) development, 21–22
Carnegie Foundation for the Advancement of
   Teaching, 30
Carnegie Initiative on the Doctorate, 7
Challenges: across phases of development,
   7–8; of Candidacy phase, 99; changing
   roles, 71–74; coursework, 46–49,
   62–63, 65; dissertation experience,
   79–81; of Entry phase, 7; examinations,
   70–71; Integration phase, 96; isolation,
   82; job search, 83–85, 100–101;
   transitions, 53–54, 85–87

Chicano students, 34
Class formats, 51–52
Cognitive development, 26–27, 28, 62–63,
   64
Cognitive-structural development, 17, 103
Collaborative learning, 94
College versus university, 4
Commitment, 27–28
Competence development, 19, 63
Comprehension development, 73–75
Conceptualizing student development,
   17–18
Conditions for development, 7
Conformity, 24–25
Council of Graduate Schools, 2, 6, 11, 29,
   31, 39, 45, 57, 70, 71, 79, 81, 99
Council on Postsecondary Education, 3
Coursework, 30, 46–49, 62, 65, 94, 96–97

D

Degree designations, 29–30
Demographics of doctoral degree students,
   32–39
Departures: attrition rates, 2–4; in
   Candidacy phase, 87–88; in Entry
   phase, 59–60; in Integration phase,
   74–75; reasons for, 11; success and, 103
Development model: overview, 8–13 (*See
   also* Phase I: Entry; Phase II: Integration;
   Phase III: Candidacy); defining, 15–18;
   diversity/differences, 11–13; historic
   aspects, 1–2; identity development, 8,
   10–11; need for understanding, 2–4;

process of, 7–8; student departure, 11, 103; three-phase concept, 8–9
Developmental research. *See* future research implications
Developmental stages, 18–21
Disabilities, students with, 37–38
Disciplinary differences, 38–39, 80–81
Dissertation advisors, 82–83
Dissertation experience, 79–82, 100
Dissertations, 30
Dissonance, 25
Diversity, 11–13
Doctoral degree designations, 29–30
Doctoral degrees: key constituencies in programs, 39–40; overview and history of U.S., 31–39; purposes of, 29–30; structure of programs, 30–31
Doctoral students, 4–7
Duality, 27

E

Ego development, 50–51
Emersion, 25
Emotional development stages, 19–21
Employment search challenges, 83–85, 100–101
Enrollment demographics, 32–39
Entry. *See* development model; Phase I: Entry
Environment, role of, 12
Epistemological development, 62–63
Ethical development stages, 19–21
Evolution of student development theory, 16–17
Examinations, 30, 70–71, 98

F

Faculty relationships, 39, 55, 57–59
Failure, 3. *See also* departures
Families of students, 39
Feedback to students, 94, 100
First-generation students, 37
Formation process, 7
Future research implications: adult development, 102; campus-environment dynamics, 103; cognitive-structural development, 103; main areas of,

101–102; professional development, 103; psychosocial development, 102; social identity development, 102; student departure and success, 103

H

Hang-over identity, 43–44

I

Identity development: across the phases of development, 10–11; conceptual framework, 8; establishing identity, 20; hang-over identity, 43–44; People of Color Racial Identity Model, 24–25; professional, 55, 86; racial, 24–25; social, 12, 24, 52–53, 102
Immersion, 25
Independence development, 54–55, 65
Infancy stage of development, 18
Integrated awareness, 25–26
Integration. *See* development model; Phase II: Integration
Integrity, development of, 20
Interdependence, 20
Internalization, 25
International students, 35
Interpersonal development stages, 19–21
Interpersonal relationships, 20
Isolation, 78, 82

J

Job search challenges, 83–85, 100–101

L

Latino students, 34
Life span stages of development, 18–21, 22

M

Married students, 36–37
Mentors, 69–79. *See also* advisor relationships
Middle-age adult stage of development, 19
Morrill Acts, 32–33
Multiplicity, 27

N

National Center for Education Statistics, 33, 34, 38
National Research Council, 6
National Science Board, 3, 34
National Science Foundation, 3, 34, 35
Nontraditional students, 36

O

Older adult stage of development, 19
Older students, 36
Orientation programs, 44–46, 93

P

Part-time students, 35–36, 58–59, 86
Peer relationships, 39, 55, 56–57, 65–66, 97
People of Color Racial Identity Model, 24–25
Phase I: Entry: about, 9–10, 41–42; assistantships, 94–95; balancing life responsibilities in, 95; changes in thinking, 49–53; cognitive development, 60, 64; coursework, 46–49, 94; departure in, 59–60; faculty relationships, 55, 57–59; forming relationships, 92–93; initial transition, 41–44; orientation, 44–46; peer relationships, 55, 56–57; self-consideration, 95–96; tasks/issues of, 92; transitioning to, 41–44, 92–94; undergraduate to graduate school transitions, 53–54
Phase II: Integration: about, 9, 10, 61–62; advisor relationship in, 97–98; changing roles, 71–74, 98–99; cognitive development, 64; coursework, 62, 65, 96–97; examinations, 70–71, 98; peer relationships, 65–66, 97; student departure in, 74–75; support during, 66–70; tasks/challenges of, 96; transitions during, 72–73
Phase III: Candidacy: about, 9, 10, 77; challenges and issues of, 99; dissertation advisors, 82–83; dissertation experience, 79–82, 100; isolation, 82; job search challenges, 83–85, 100–101; professional role, transition to, 85–87, 101; student departure in, 87–88; transition to, 78–79, 99–100
Phases of development. *See* development model
Preschooler stage of development, 18
Professional (career) development, 21–22, 73–74, 101
Professional development, 103
Professional identity, 55
Professional role, transition to, 85–87, 101
Psychosocial development, 12, 17, 18–21, 53, 55, 102
Purpose, development of, 20

R

Racial identity development, 24–26
Recipients of doctoral degrees, 31–32
Relationships: advisor, 66–70, 97–98; colleagues/workplace, 40; establishing new, 95–96; faculty, 55, 57–59; forming, 92–93; interpersonal, 20; peer, 55, 56–57, 65–66, 93, 97
Relativism, 27
Research: on doctoral programs, 4–7, 105–106; future implication, 101–103; on students, 1–4
Responsibilities, 95
Role continuance, 21
Roles: advisory, 68, 82; changing, 63–64, 65, 71–74, 98–99; of environment, 12; non-student, 5; professional, 85–87; steward of the discipline, 86; terminology for describing, 67

S

Scholarship areas in doctoral education, 6
School-age stage of development, 18
Sciences, technology, engineering, and mathematics (STEM) disciplines, 34, 35, 37
Self-awareness, 4, 49–50
Self-consideration, 95–96
Self-direction, 65

Social consequences of attrition, 3–4
Social development, 12
Social identity development, 17, 24, 26, 52–53, 102
STEM (sciences, technology, engineering, and mathematics) disciplines, 34, 35, 36, 37, 38
Steward of the discipline role, 86
Student departures. *See* departures
Student development. *See* development model; future research implications
Students of color, 34–35, 53
Students with disabilities, 37–38
Support. *See also* relationships: advisor relationships, 66–67, 82–83; in Integration phase, 66–70; orientation in Entry phase, 44–46; peer relationships, 65–66; relationships, 55–59
Survey of Earned Doctorates, 29

T

Tasks of life stage development, 18–21; Candidacy phase, 99; Entry phase of development, 92; Integration phase, 96
Thesis. *See* dissertations
Thinking, changes in, 49–53
Three-phase concept, 8–9
Time-to-completion of dissertation, 87–88

Time-to-degree rates, 31
Toddler stage of development, 18
Transformational work, 86–87
Transitions, life stage, 23
Transitions to/in developmental stages: Candidacy phase, 78–79, 99–100; in Entry phase, 41–44, 92–94; Phase II, 72; transition theory, 43–44; undergraduate to graduate school, 53–54

U

U.S. Department of Education, 34, 38
University of Chicago, 101
University versus college, 4

V

Vectors of psychosocial development, 19–21

W

Women, 33–34, 53
Working students, 39–40
Workload management, 48–49

Y

Young adult stage of development, 19

About the Author

Susan K. Gardner began her career as a high school Spanish teacher in Alma Center, Wisconsin. During her five years in this position, she worked part time to earn her master's degree in teaching from the University of Wisconsin, La Crosse. Upon graduating in 2001, she sought employment in higher education, hoping to work with students in leadership positions, and found a position at Washington State University in Pullman. While in that position, she found her passion for higher education and began working part time on her Ph.D. in higher education–student affairs. She became a full-time student in 2003 to pursue a position as a faculty member. Working as a research assistant for the Carnegie Initiative on the Doctorate in the College of Education, she learned about doctoral education as she experienced it. This initial experience prompted her current work on doctoral education, which seeks to understand the contexts and cultures that foster success for doctoral students. After earning her Ph.D. in 2005, she began her academic career at Louisiana State University. In 2007, she and her husband moved to Maine, where she is now assistant professor of higher education at the University of Maine.

About the ASHE Higher Education Report Series

Since 1983, the ASHE (formerly ASHE-ERIC) Higher Education Report Series has been providing researchers, scholars, and practitioners with timely and substantive information on the critical issues facing higher education. Each monograph presents a definitive analysis of a higher education problem or issue, based on a thorough synthesis of significant literature and institutional experiences. Topics range from planning to diversity and multiculturalism, to performance indicators, to curricular innovations. The mission of the Series is to link the best of higher education research and practice to inform decision making and policy. The reports connect conventional wisdom with research and are designed to help busy individuals keep up with the higher education literature. Authors are scholars and practitioners in the academic community. Each report includes an executive summary, review of the pertinent literature, descriptions of effective educational practices, and a summary of key issues to keep in mind to improve educational policies and practice.

The Series is one of the most peer reviewed in higher education. A National Advisory Board made up of ASHE members reviews proposals. A National Review Board of ASHE scholars and practitioners reviews completed manuscripts. Six monographs are published each year and they are approximately 120 pages in length. The reports are widely disseminated through Jossey-Bass and John Wiley & Sons, and they are available online to subscribing institutions through Wiley InterScience (http://www.interscience.wiley.com).

Call for Proposals

The ASHE Higher Education Report Series is actively looking for proposals. We encourage you to contact one of the editors, Dr. Kelly Ward (kaward@wsu.edu) or Dr. Lisa Wolf-Wendel (lwolf@ku.edu), with your ideas.

Recent Titles

ASHE HIGHER EDUCATION REPORT
Order Form
SUBSCRIPTIONS AND SINGLE ISSUES

DISCOUNTED BACK ISSUES:

Use this form to receive **20% off** all back issues of ASHE Higher Education Report. All single issues priced at **$23.20** (normally $29.00)

TITLE	ISSUE NO.	ISBN
_____	_____	_____
_____	_____	_____
_____	_____	_____

Call 888-378-2537 or see mailing instructions below. When calling, mention the promotional code, JB7ND, to receive your discount.

SUBSCRIPTIONS: *(1 year, 6 issues)*

☐ New Order   ☐ Renewal

U.S.	☐ Individual: $174	☐ Institutional: $228
Canada/Mexico	☐ Individual: $174	☐ Institutional: $288
All Others	☐ Individual: $210	☐ Institutional: $339

Call 888-378-2537 or see mailing and pricing instructions below. Online subscriptions are available at www.interscience.wiley.com.

Copy or detach page and send to:
John Wiley & Sons, Journals Dept., 5th Floor
989 Market Street, San Francisco, CA 94103-1741
Order Form can also be faxed to: 888-481-2665

Issue/Subscription Amount: $ _____
Shipping Amount: $ _____
(for single issues only—subscription prices include shipping)
Total Amount: $ _____

SHIPPING CHARGES:

SURFACE	Domestic	Canadian
First Item	$5.00	$6.00
Each Add'l Item	$3.00	$1.50

[No sales tax for U.S. subscriptions. Canadian residents, add GST for subscription orders. Individual rate subscriptions must be paid by personal check or credit card. Individual rate subscriptions may not be resold as library copies.]

☐ Payment enclosed (U.S. check or money order only. All payments must be in U.S. dollars.)

☐ VISA ☐ MC ☐ Amex # _____ Exp. Date _____

Card Holder Name _____ Card Issue # _____

Signature_____ Day Phone _____

☐ Bill Me (U.S. institutional orders only. Purchase order required.)

Purchase order # _____
Federal Tax ID13559302   GST 89102 8052

Name_____

Address _____

Phone _____ E-mail _____

JB7ND

ASHE-ERIC HIGHER EDUCATION REPORT IS NOW AVAILABLE ONLINE AT WILEY INTERSCIENCE

What is Wiley InterScience?

Wiley InterScience is the dynamic online content service from John Wiley & Sons delivering the full text of over 300 leading scientific, technical, medical, and professional journals, plus major reference works, the acclaimed Current Protocols laboratory manuals, and even the full text of select Wiley print books online.

What are some special features of Wiley InterScience?

Wiley Interscience Alerts is a service that delivers table of contents via e-mail for any journal available on Wiley InterScience as soon as a new issue is published online.

Early View is Wiley's exclusive service presenting individual articles online as soon as they are ready, even before the release of the compiled print issue. These articles are complete, peer-reviewed, and citable.

CrossRef is the innovative multi-publisher reference linking system enabling readers to move seamlessly from a reference in a journal article to the cited publication, typically located on a different server and published by a different publisher.

How can I access Wiley InterScience?

Visit http://www.interscience.wiley.com.

Guest Users can browse Wiley InterScience for unrestricted access to journal Tables of Contents and Article Abstracts, or use the powerful search engine.
Registered Users are provided with a *Personal Home Page* to store and manage customized alerts, searches, and links to favorite journals and articles. Additionally, Registered Users can view free Online Sample Issues and preview selected material from major reference works.
Licensed Customers are entitled to access full-text journal articles in PDF, with select journals also offering full-text HTML.

How do I become an Authorized User?

Authorized Users are individuals authorized by a paying Customer to have access to the journals in Wiley InterScience. For example, a University that subscribes to Wiley journals is considered to be the Customer.

Faculty, staff and students authorized by the University to have access to those journals in Wiley InterScience are Authorized Users. Users should contact their Library for information on which Wiley journals they have access to in Wiley InterScience.

ASK YOUR INSTITUTION ABOUT WILEY INTERSCIENCE TODAY!

.